ONLINE PROFESSIONAL DEVELOPMENT
THROUGH VIRTUAL LEARNING COMMUNITIES

RC
OT
Royal College of
Occupational
Therapists

ONLINE PROFESSIONAL DEVELOPMENT
THROUGH **VIRTUAL LEARNING COMMUNITIES**

SONJA HOLLINS-ALEXANDER

CORWIN
A SAGE Company

CORWIN
A SAGE Company

FOR INFORMATION

Corwin
A SAGE Company
2455 Teller Road
Thousand Oaks, California 91320
(800) 233-9936
www.corwin.com

SAGE Publications Ltd.
1 Oliver's Yard
55 City Road
London, EC1Y 1SP
United Kingdom

SAGE Publications India Pvt. Ltd.
B 1/I 1 Mohan Cooperative Industrial Area
Mathura Road, New Delhi 110 044
India

SAGE Publications Asia-Pacific Pte. Ltd.
3 Church Street
#10-04 Samsung Hub
Singapore 049483

Acquisitions Editor: Dan Alpert
Associate Editor: Kimberly Greenberg
Editorial Assistant: Heidi Arndt
Permissions Editor: Karen Ehrmann
Production Editor: Veronica Stapleton Hooper
Copy Editor: Kim Husband
Typesetter: Hurix Systems Private Ltd.
Proofreader: Joyce Li
Indexer: Molly Hall
Cover Designer: Anupama Krishnan

Printed in the United States of America.

Library of Congress Cataloging-in-Publication Data

Hollins-Alexander, Sonja.
Online professional development through virtual learning communities / Sonja Hollins-Alexander.

pages cm
Includes bibliographical references and index.

ISBN 978-1-4522-7666-3 (pbk.)

1. Teachers—In-service training—Computer networks. 2. Professional learning communities. I. Title.

LB1731.H59 2013

370.71'1—dc23

2013005340

This book is printed on acid-free paper.

MIX
Paper from
responsible sources
FSC www.fsc.org **FSC® C014174**

13 14 15 16 17 10 9 8 7 6 5 4 3 2 1

Contents

Preface

The Evolution of a Design

Five years ago when I transitioned into my position as director of professional learning for a large urban district, it became and continues to be my passion to support schools and the educators in my district with high-quality professional learning. There was little to no specificity for how to accomplish this daunting and exhilarating task for a person who had been in a central office position for only 3 months. Therefore, I really had to depend on my previous experiences to guide me. I had previously served in the capacity of teacher, school social worker, assistant principal, principal, and assistant director, with 11 years as an administrator. Through those lenses, I had a good idea of what quality professional learning should feel like at the end of the day and what it should look like in practice. Those critical positions afforded me opportunities to design professional learning at my worksites for colleagues, and on several occasions, I was provided an opportunity to share my levels of expertise with colleagues outside of my worksite.

As an administrator, my keen skill was that of providing resources for those I supported, and for me, the greatest resource in support of them being effective in their positions was quality adult learning experiences. I found that the experiences were richer when this work was done collaboratively with colleagues and they moved from their isolated areas of expertise and shared their talents with each other. As a building administrator, it was rare that I would use my small pot of funds to bring in a consultant on staff development days. I found it more beneficial to have the staff learn from each other. Since I was privileged to have knowledge of everyone's skills as the principal, I knew a little secret that they did not know about each other that I believed would be beneficial to them all. That secret was their qualifications, talents, and passions for a variety of teaching strategies. I had all the expertise that was needed to prepare and support an effective staff. I needed to provide them an effective format in which they could share their collective talents. Back in the days before I even knew the term *professional learning communities*, I started to build community around the learning goals of the staff in my building. Perhaps my background as a social worker has always led me to support the interconnectedness that humans thrive from, and creating those structures in my school environments through professional learning was always my desire. Over the years as an administrator, I saw the power of me and my staff learning together in teams and building off the knowledge that was collectively shared through these experiences.

When given the opportunity as a district leader in the Department of Professional Learning, I was determined to recreate this feeling of interconnectedness, this practice of learning from each other, from other schools, and other educators. It was my way of extending my territory. However, I had a serious barrier to this type of structure. As I set forth on this journey, there was one barrier that would allow me to physically impact only a few educators due to the size of the district and the human resources that were afforded to me to get the job done. I serve a district of more than 13,000 employees, with approximately 7,000 of them being classroom teachers. From the northernmost end to the southern tip, we are geographically 246 square miles. The essential question was, "How could I accomplish this type of learning experience" with more than 7,000 teachers, 5 staff members, and a dwindling budget.

Soon after my feet hit the ground running as the director of the department and I was given the opportunity to set some goals and move full speed ahead, I started to research viable options for extending the opportunity of high-quality professional learning experiences with a focus on learning communities. I took my team of five and assigned them approximately 30 schools to support. Their task was to connect with the principals and offer them an opportunity to take their staff through a process of team development and focused professional learning centered on their school's data and goals. Along the way, there was a great amount of research being done on this novel idea of "professional learning communities." Wow, I think I now understood and had a model for my grassroots effort to bring my teachers together years ago. How grand it would be if I could do this across the entire district. I was excited, I was ambitious, and I was ready to go spread the gospel about these professional learning communities to every principal who would allow us to knock on the door and partner up with the staff.

As great as this idea was, after about 10 months of this spreading like wildfire and getting the principals engaged around this great idea, I realized a few things. I realized that I would never be able to provide this face-to-face service to all 146 schools in the district within the next 5-year cycle. I realized that I was wearing my team down and they were not able to focus on any of the other equally important initiatives we were implementing out of the department. I realized that I had to think of another viable option to build capacity for this type of learning for educators while at the same time making sure it was sustained after we walked out the door.

Over the past 3 years, some major shifts occurred in my quest to extend this valuable opportunity of learning to more and more educators through building capacity and sustainable structures. It has been a true evolution to what is now the most viable option. As I set out on the journey for this option, I tried a few structures of supporting my desire to implement professional learning communities in schools. I was fortunate enough to partner with the experts in the area of professional learning community. Several years ago, I hosted a session in the district with the Dufours through video conferencing. I recall thinking how powerful it was to use this technology tool and provide learning around this concept in an auditorium to more than 500 educators. In addition, 2 years ago, I was also able to engage in a Professional Learning

Communities Institute with Shirley Hord, Bill Sommers, and Jim Roussin. They visited our district on five occasions throughout that year and spent 2 to 3 days with my team and teams of educators. They engaged my team and 11 principals and their teams through a yearlong intensive study on the implementation of professional learning communities. These principals, teacher leaders, and district leaders have now been utilized in the district as resident experts and have presented at local conferences for large groups of other teachers and administrators in the district. Through these extensive learning opportunities, my team and I developed a curriculum in support of guiding schools with the implementation of professional learning communities. We spent time visiting schools, but in addition, we hosted a weekly webinar, providing each school the tools to engage in this virtual opportunity while remaining at their school site. All of these attempts led me closer to understanding the power of technology to bring large groups together.

We ventured out over the past few years to incorporating online learning opportunities for our educators. This is when I could really see how I would build capacity for high-quality learning structures in the district. Originally, we used ready-made online courses from vendors, and we gave teachers access to enroll in those courses. However, we were not fully satisfied because these valuable opportunities were not always aligned to the needs of our teachers and our district. There was always something missing or added that we did not need. We researched the opportunities to design and develop our own courses. It was this process that led us to develop a process of engagement for participants that supported the concepts of professional learning communities. You will learn about this process as you read this book.

Over the years, I have had the freedom to truly set a vision for what I believed was necessary for the educators in my district to aspire to and remain effective in their roles through targeted adult learning experiences. This process has evolved over time as I have grown and been able to partner with an online course designer, Mrs. Henderson-Rosser, and a team of quality facilitators to be the conduit of delivering on the promise of high-quality professional learning experiences. As we have transitioned to using online structures for learning, it has always been imperative from the start to take high-quality face-to-face professional learning opportunities and offer them to teachers in their own spaces, places, and times for learning. As this virtual structure of learning is developed and designed, which is now termed the *PLeCampus*, the national standards of professional development were and will remain at the forefront of each course and opportunity offered to teachers. As well, course development in the virtual professional learning community supports the Joyce and Showers (1980) model for what is needed for good professional development.

Ultimately, I would like for the learners in the district to know that there is a partnership that exists between them and other learners in the courses they take or in their schools and other schools. It is my belief that the second-order change will ultimately be seen in the students they support. I want them to know through experience how 2, 3, 30, or even 100 educators can engage in high-powered solution-oriented conversations, collective thinking, collaboration, and planning sessions in virtual learning communities (VLCs) in support of them obtaining exemplary and pervasive student achievement results through this high-quality professional learning experience.

This model of learning has actualized into the Learner–Learner model, which fully supports a symbiotic relationship among learners in a community. It is my desire, passion, and responsibility to execute the design of the Learner–Learner model of professional learning experiences so that this type of interaction can occur. It is my hope that you will read about our journey and can use this model and structure to provide this level of learning and interconnectedness to those you support. What is so very powerful is that wherever you may be, through technology in VLCs, we can always have opportunities to learn from each other. What a way to extend our territory and impact the field of teaching and learning like we have never been able to do before!

Acknowledgments

Always giving honor and appreciation to God is what keeps me focused and moving in the direction that I was destined to go. My daughter Autumn's quest for knowledge and love of learning is the face that I see when I seek to provide opportunities for the educators she and millions of other growing young minds will depend upon for a better future. Autumn motivates me to be my very best because that is what she deserves and more. My mother, Mildred, and my deceased father, John, will always be my greatest inspiration to never stop my quest for the best life has to offer me and living out my passion. My sisters and brothers, Teresa, Jane, John, and Earl, and all of my family who encapsulate me with love and encouragement no matter what endeavor I seek to accomplish, and my dearest best friend, Michael, who would not let me give up on accomplishing this goal, and through his love and encouragement gave me a vision when I was too tired to see it.

I have a host of friends and coworkers in addition to my contributors (Debra, Jermain, Lakissa, LaTonya, Morcease, and the entire PL Department) that are too many to name but all instrumental in my meeting this goal. I thank each of you for that listening ear that never was closed to me discussing my dreams. I want to thank my business partner and friend, Aleigha, who is foundational for me and this work. I had a vision and a plan, but she has the ideas and the skill. Through her, I have learned so much about technology, and because she is the teacher and creator that she is, she has opened our future to a world of possibilities that are just starting to bloom. I want to thank one of my mentors, Marcia Tate, who provided me so much encouragement and support and has always been a role model that I look up to as a writer and leader in professional development.

Finally, I want to thank my awesome editor, Dan (who always believed in me, even when I did not believe in myself), and the family at Corwin (Mike S., Melissa, Monique, and Mike G.). You never gave up on me! I am forever grateful for your encouragement, motivation, and the opportunity of my life-time to actualize on my dream and passion as a writer.

Publisher's Acknowledgments

Corwin gratefully acknowledges the contributions of the following reviewers:

Susan Bolte
Principal, Providence Elementary
Aubrey, TX

Catherine Huber
Principal, Northwood Elementary
West Seneca, NY

Nancy Kellogg
Education Consultant
Boulder, CO

Jennifer W. Ramamoorthi
Building Assistant, Community Consolidated School District 59
Mount Prospect, IL

About the Author

Dr. Sonja Hollins-Alexander has been in the field of education for 22 years, with 16 of those in educational leadership at the school, district, and higher-education levels. During this time, she has served as a school social worker, teacher, assistant principal, principal, and assistant director and currently serves as a the director of professional learning for a large urban school district. She also is a professor in the Education Department at Argosy University–Atlanta and Troy University–Covington. Through her professional journey, she has had experiences in strategic planning, organizational improvement, policy development, project and program management, stakeholder communication and engagement, budget planning, grant writing, instructional design, curriculum development and implementation, facilitation of adult learning, conference facilitation and design, quality assurance team member for AdvancED, and fully engaged in the development and use of online collaborative/instructional software.

She has a proven ability at leading and establishing quality partnerships with highly effective teams and a history of leading teams to increased student achievement and enhanced teacher quality. While she served as principal, Dr. Hollins-Alexander's school received the 2006 Gold Award for Greatest Gain in Percentage of Students Meeting and Exceeding Standards from the Georgia Office of Student Achievement, the Georgia Department of Education, and the governor. She has led numerous school teams through the implementation of site-based collaboration structures such as PLCs, whole-faculty study groups, and critical friends groups to develop initiatives that will improve standards-based learning for students and performance development for teachers and leaders.

These experiences have led her to many opportunities to present on a local and national level on the following topics: "Engaging Parents—Chesnut Charter School Online K–12 Ambit Process"; "The Creative Enrichment Learning Laboratory—A Schoolwide Enrichment Model"; "Building Sustainability and Capacity Through Online Professional Development"; "The Strategic Route to Instructional and Organizational Excellence: A Step-by-Step Guide to a District's Unique Quality-Improvement Process"; and "Whole-Faculty Study Groups—A District's Journey to Implementing Professional Learning Communities." Dr. Hollins-Alexander has received a state award for being a distinguished principal and the Learning Forward National Shirley Havens Classified Employees Staff Development Award. She has served on numerous community and professional boards of directors and has a passion for leading the work of personal development and professional growth with a focus on educators. She is currently the president-elect for the Georgia Learning Forward Board of Directors.

Dr. Hollins-Alexander's leadership experiences have prepared her for 21st-century leadership. While serving in her current capacity, she supports more than 13,000 employees, and determining methods for building capacity, sustainability, and scalability without compromising quality and collaboration is a must. Therefore, 3 years ago, she and her team instituted the PLeCampus, a collaborative online community of customized professional development courses. This work was featured in an article titled "One Stop PD Shop" in ISTE's *Leading and*

Learning With Technology June 2010 issue. As she continues on this journey, she will provide you full insight into this work led by her and implemented by committed skilled professionals in the field of education with a passion for technology. Dr. Hollins-Alexander is chief operations officer for Learning Centric, LLC, and may be reached at salexander@learningcentricllc.com.

About the Contributors

 **Mrs. Aleigha Henderson-Rosser** has more than 17 years of educational experience. She has served as a middle school science teacher, instructional technology specialist, and founder of the DeKalb Online Academy. She has served as a coordinator of professional learning, overseeing the design, creation, and implementation of the PLeCampus and additional face-to-face professional learning opportunities for more than 13,000 employees and, most recently she was promoted to director of instructional technology in Atlanta Public Schools.

Mrs. Henderson-Rosser is currently studying instructional technology and online course design in the educational leadership doctoral program at Georgia State University. Her international and national involvement in the technology community consists of serving as founding member and board member of the International Association for K–12 Online Learning (iNACoL)–Georgia chapter, member of Learning Forward (formerly National Staff Development Council), member of the International Society for Technology in Education, and member of the International Forum for Women in e-Learning (IFWE).

Mrs. Henderson-Rosser was recently published in the June 2010 ISTE publication *Leading and Learning With Technology* in a feature article titled "One Stop PD Shop," which focused on the implementation of online professional learning in a large urban district. She has been a featured conference presenter at the AdvancED International Conference, International Society for Technology in Education (ISTE) Conference, Georgia Educational Technology Conference, National Staff Development Conference, and the Teachscape Leadership Conference.

She is excited to lead the work of learning in a digital age and is currently leading initiatives around creating innovative teacher leaders, online professional learning for instructional technology, impact of instructional technology on teaching and learning, and the implementation of 21st-century teaching and learning through digitally connected classrooms. Mrs. Henderson-Rosser is chief information officer for Learning Centric, LLC.

Mrs. Tanya R. Ogletree has more than 20 years' experience in the field of education.

Mrs. Ogletree began her career as a paraprofessional, later completing certification and becoming a classroom teacher. Upon completion of her educational specialist degree in educational leadership, Mrs. Ogletree transitioned into a teacher leader position with the Department of Professional Learning. This position afforded her an opportunity to utilize skills and knowledge obtained from a master's degree in educational technology. Mrs. Ogletree has served as a facilitator for face-to-face courses, blended-model courses, and online courses. Mrs. Ogletree has also provided trainings and workshops on technology implementation and integration.

Mrs. Natasha Rachell has served in the field of education for 9 years and is extremely passionate about educating both children and teachers. She believes that merging professional development and technology is the way of the future and allows career educators the opportunity to continue to grow both their professional and personal toolboxes in an effort to make them more effective in their practices. Mrs. Rachell has served as a high school science teacher, professional learning coach, and educational technology specialist. She prides herself on establishing positive relationships among those that she interacts with and feels that once this is done, a trust is built that allows for the work and the learning to take place. It is her personal educational philosophy that all children can and will learn if and only if they have the right teacher in front of them in the right place and at the right time. She strives to be a lifelong learner herself and knows that if she wants to see education move forward to produce 21st-century learners, she needs to live and be the change that she wishes to see. Mrs. Rachell lives in Decatur, Georgia, with her husband, Melvin, and sons, Elijah and Jacob.

Mrs. Melissa Dandy Walker is a passionate, proactive educator who is an advocate for the power of online professional development. She has been in the field of education for 16 years and has varied experience in education, including the roles of math teacher/department chair, math coach, professional learning coach, online math instructor, professional learning instructor (face-to-face, online, and blended courses), and, most recently, digital learning specialist. Mrs. Walker has been an online professional learning instructor for the last 5 years, and through that experience, she has come to realize the power of positive relationships. Building relationships is just as important online as it is in face-to-face courses, and the Learner–Learner model can be a catalyst for deeper learning and understanding. Mrs. Walker and the participants in her online courses learn as much from interacting with one another as they do from the content in the course. She resides in Rex, Georgia, with her husband, Jerry, and sons, Jordan and Noah.

1

The Learner–Learner Model

The Learner–Learner model was a term that evolved out of planning and developing the district's design for a professional learning virtual campus. The model supports the design and structure of a community of continuous shared learning in a collaborative culture of professional development. The Learner–Learner model is based on the tenets of Vygotsky's social constructivist theory (1978) and the constructs of andragogy (Knowles, 1980).

The Learner–Learner model supports learning in all environments; however, in a computing Web-based learning community, this model enables learners to collaboratively co-construct meaning of concepts using technology as a conduit for shared knowledge development. This experience is enhanced when the technology supports a collaboration platform and professional learning activity that provide the organizational and process structure that brings two or more participants together to learn through shared decision making, peer interactions, reflections, and performance expectations (see Figure 1A). Thus, the tenets of

Figure 1A

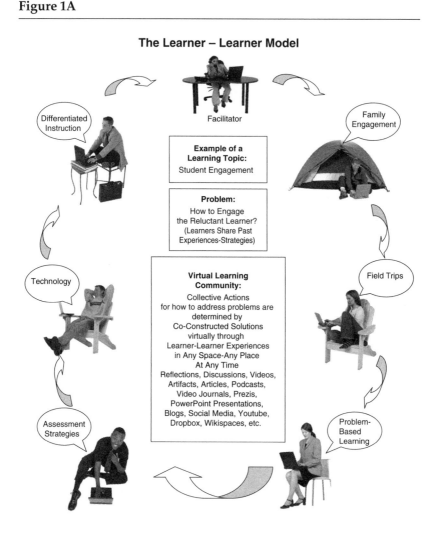

The Learner – Learner Model

Facilitator

Differentiated Instruction

Family Engagement

Example of a Learning Topic:
Student Engagement

Problem:
How to Engage
the Reluctant Learner?
(Learners Share Past
Experiences-Strategies)

Technology

Field Trips

Virtual Learning Community:
Collective Actions
for how to address problems are
determined by
Co-Constructed Solutions
virtually through
Learner-Learner Experiences
in Any Space-Any Place
At Any Time
Reflections, Discussions, Videos,
Artifacts, Articles, Podcasts,
Video Journals, Prezis,
PowerPoint Presentations,
Blogs, Social Media, Youtube,
Dropbox, Wikispaces, etc.

Assessment Strategies

Problem-Based Learning

this model support the social constructivist theory, the concepts of andragogy, and the development of a learning community within the actual and virtual classroom.

SECTION TWO: WHAT IS SOCIAL CONSTRUCTIVISM?

Social constructivism emphasizes the importance of culture and context in understanding what occurs in society and constructing knowledge based on this understanding (Derry, 1999;

McMahon, 1997). Instructional models based on the social constructivist perspective stress the need for collaboration among learners and with practitioners in the society (Lave & Wenger, 1991; McMahon, 1997). Lave and Wenger (1991) assert that a society's practical knowledge is situated in relations among practitioners, their practice, and the social organization and political economy of communities of practice. Their model of situated learning proposed that learning involved a process of engagement in a community of practice. For this reason, learning should involve such knowledge and practice (Gredler, 1997; Lave & Wenger, 1991). Social constructivist approaches can include reciprocal teaching, peer collaboration, cognitive apprenticeships, problem-based instruction, webquests, anchored instruction, and other methods that involve learning with others (Schunk, 2000). Social constructivism is based on specific assumptions about reality, knowledge, and learning.

> **Reality:** Social constructivists believe that reality is constructed through human activity. Members of a society together invent the properties of the world (Kukla, 2000). For the social constructivist, reality cannot be discovered: It does not exist prior to its social invention.

> **Knowledge:** To social constructivists, knowledge is also a human product and is socially and culturally constructed (Ernest, 1999; Gredler, 1997; Prawat & Floden, 1994). Individuals create meaning through their interactions with each other and with the environment they live in.

> **Learning:** Social constructivists view learning as a social process. It does not take place only within an individual, nor is it a passive development of behaviors that are shaped by external forces (McMahon, 1997). Meaningful learning occurs when individuals are engaged in social activities.

Social Constructivism as a Theory That Supports Professional Development

Social constructivist theory is rooted in the interaction of two or more people. More specifically, it supports peer collaboration and learning that is viewed as a social process. The tenets of this theory are a basis for educators continuing to enhance the profession through socially constructed activities in a learning community. Through structured professional development activities of two or more people, educators are guided through reflective practice and deep thinking. This type of professional development is a powerful approach to promote teacher learning. Peer collaboration requires discussion, reflection, and observation. This type of teacher learning encourages an active role for each participant in the learning community.

Too often, professional development structures are designed such that the teacher has a passive role; the term most frequently used is *sit and get*. Though these sessions provide valuable information about strategies, the teacher as the learner has a passive role and is often unable to engage in deep reflective conversation with a peer or the presenter in support of how this information will be transferred into skill development and, ultimately, the classroom environment. Researchers have made numerous reflections in the field of professional development on measuring impact that have highlighted the ineffectiveness of "sit and get." This type of learning environment does not support peer collaboration or the engaging interaction of conversation or collaboration among teachers and has thereby been determined ineffective in producing transformational change among teachers' knowledge, skills, or behaviors.

Professional development should be designed based upon brain research and learning style theory with the implementation of strategies that facilitate comprehension and retention (Tate, 2004. Dr. Tate identifies several strategies in her publication *Sit and Get Won't Grow Dendrites: 20 Professional Learning Strategies That Engage the Adult Brain*, such as:

- brainstorming and discussion
- project-based and problem-based instruction
- reciprocal teaching, cooperative learning, and peer coaching
- visuals
- writing

Learners should be active participants. Only when professional developers engage them in the process of learning through engaging strategies will we see the results we seek to improve and enhance teacher learning and teaching quality. This is a non-negotiable aspect of high-quality professional development. Interaction and engagement are key to adult learning! But they must be meaningful and relevant.

Teacher learning is supported by all aspects of learning theory. Learning is an active and intellectual process; therefore, it is important for the teacher to be the one doing the intellectual work (Danielson, 2009). Reflective dialogue with peers about practice using analytical and evaluative skills requires teachers to examine the instructional decisions they make that contribute to the process of thinking and learning (Danielson, 2009). However, the role of another person is critical. The social process of learning with others allows for the two to construct meaning and enhance the body of knowledge about teacher practices and effective use of new skills that are learned in a professional-development activity. Thus, in the Learner–Learner model, this process is considered the roadmap to creating a symbiotic relationship between peers and co-construction of knowledge in support of improved practice. This is enhanced in professional-development activities that are guided by clear standards of practice, and the collaboration, peer feedback, and reflection should be executed against the learning standards of the professional-development activity. This process provides the structure to close the professional learning and performance gaps that impede teacher effectiveness and support the opportunity for the teacher (learner) and facilitator (learner) in a professional-development activity to move toward the teacher's quest to strengthen and develop her or his skills around the standard of learning for that activity.

Too often, teachers participate in quality learning experiences, but there is no opportunity to follow up, practice, or continue to engage with others around the new learning. In the Learner–Learner model, the facilitator learns from the teachers as the teachers learn from each other and the facilitator. The learning activity is continuous and is not isolated to one setting, at one time, in one place, with sometimes only one opportunity to learn form each other. In the Learner–Learner model, the learning process threads through all members in an active and ongoing cycle of engagement, feedback, and reflection, as noted in Figure 1A. Knowledge is shared and continues to flow through the participants and the facilitator using the power and magic of technology! The facilitator orchestrates the environment for this type of learning to occur using a variety of tools and resources that foster engagement, feedback, and reflection among all the learners in the community. This co-constructed reflection and feedback enables the participants to develop meaning and understanding against standards and ultimately improve their practice, which is the goal of any quality professional-development activity. No longer do learners work in isolation or solve problems in silos. Learners come together and develop solutions together throughout the learning activity with other learners who have experienced or will experience similar challenges. They are able to co-construct strategies to improve practice and impact student learning. This level of engagement enhances the power of social constructivist principles in professional-development activities.

SECTION THREE: WHAT IS ANDRAGOGY AND HOW DOES IT SUPPORT THE LEARNER–LEARNER MODEL?

Andragogy is said to be rooted in the approaches of Plato and his teacher, Socrates. The term was initially used by Alexander Kapp in 1833. Kapp applied it to the necessity of lifelong learning through self-reflection as introduced by Plato. The term was used throughout Europe and eventually was introduced to a professor of adult education at Boston University, Malcolm Knowles.

The intent of the concept of andragogy was to present a shift from pedagogical approaches that were teacher directed to a learner-centered methodology in which the needs of the learner are considered and the learner collaborates with the instructor in decisions that are made about the learner's education. The role of the instructor is that of facilitator and coach instead of expert authoritarian (Bolden, 2008). Andragogy originally supported the idea that adults require unique designs for learning. It was determined to be the art and science of teaching adults how to learn by Alexander Kapp in 1833 and further developed into a full theory of adult education by Malcolm Knowles. However, in Knowles's 1980 publication, his thoughts on four of the five key assumptions of andragogy apply equally to adults and children, but children have fewer experiences and preestablished beliefs than adults do.

According to Knowles (1973), the following facets to learning listed support androgogic principles:

- Learners are problem centered rather than content centered.
- Instructors permit and encourage the active participation of the learners.
- Instructors encourage the learner to introduce past experiences into the learning process in order to reexamine those experiences in the light of new data.
- The climate of learning must be collaborative (instructor to learner and learner to learner) as opposed to authority oriented.
- The learning environment (planning, conducting, evaluating) is a mutual activity between learner and instructor.
- Evaluation leads to appraisal of needs and interests and therefore to the redesign of new learning activities.
- Activities are experimental.

Thus, the primary function of the instructor is to become a guide to the process of learning, not a manager of content. The learning guide uses two-way communication to establish the objectives and methods of the learning process.

How Does Andragogy Support the Learner–Learner Model?

Andragogy concepts support the constructs of learning being a mutual activity between the learners and the facilitator and among the learners. There is no hierarchal process through which those who know are expected and required to teach those who do not know. The climate in the Learner–Learner model is at all times based on collaboration and is social, not done in isolation. The context of learning in the Learner–Learner model supports problem identification and resolution among the learners in the community or the class. The Learner–Learner model provides for active involvement of the participants at all times. In a technology-centered environment, this can happen at any time, in any place or space. This is one of the many reasons this is such a powerful method of professional development for very busy educators who fight for time for their own learning on a constant basis.

> Learning is enhanced when it is more like a team effort than a solo race. Good learning, like good work, is collaborative and social, not competitive and isolated. Working with others often increases involvement in learning. Sharing one's ideas and responding to others improves thinking and deepens understanding.—*Chickering & Gamson, 1987, p. 1*

The Learner–Learner model encourages peer-to-peer reflections through facilitated self-directed learning experiences. It is critical that time be allotted for facilitator feedback as well as individual and peer reflection in an ongoing discussion forum in learning communities. This is the arena in which previous experiences enhance the learning and support co-constructed solutions to problems that learners face in education. The quality of effort in this reflective collaborative format combats the lack of time learners often have for their own learning when the learning is isolated. Providing a learning environment in the Learner–Learner model of learning in which colleagues can learn from each other capitalizes on the time that is lost, provides deeper levels of involvement, and enhances the learning opportunity for all in the learning community.

SECTION FOUR: THE LEARNER–LEARNER MODEL AS A BASIS FOR PROFESSIONAL LEARNING COMMUNITIES

Professional development that improves the learning of all students provides educators with the knowledge and skills to collaborate (National Staff Development Council, 2001). In a professional learning community (PLC), the vision grows as people work together and collaborate over time. The community of learners constructs a vision through shared collective decisions regarding the improvements they will work toward for the increased learning of students. Simply stated, they learn from each other in a collaborative environment, co-constructing meaning out of this experience. "Professional Learning that increases educator effectiveness and results for all students occurs within learning communities committed to continuous improvement, collective responsibility, and goal alignment" (Learning Forward, 2011, p. 24).

The Learner–Learner model supports a community of continuous, simultaneous learning and leading opportunities among learners in a collaborative culture. Through professional-development structures, this model delivers cognitive (learning) opportunities for shared concept construction and development to occur between two or more people. Roland Barth (2006) described and distinguished a culture of shared decision making by the following actions taken by teachers: talking with one another about their practice, sharing their craft knowledge, observing one another while they are engaged in practice, and rooting for one another's success.

As identified by Hord and Sommers (2009), a PLC is characterized by adult learners coming together to study collegially and work collaboratively. They are continuously learning together and applying what they have learned to their work. The major emphasis in a collaborative community is on collective learning, when individuals learn more than if they are learning independently. The PLC is not just about collaboration; it is about collaborating to learn together about a topic the community deems (*through shared collective decisions*) important. The learning is focused on effective teaching and increased student learning.

Successful learning communities build shared knowledge bases, and this knowledge contributes to enhanced possibilities for the community's vision.

The *learning* in successful learning communities is supported by collegial inquiry, enhanced through guided reflection by the participants (learners) who share dialogue about their reflection and create new knowledge to shape their craft. The conversations focus on their practice and how it impacts the students they teach. These conversations can be initiated through discussion prompts by which participants are asked and share with others how their learning influences their teaching practices, which affects student learning outcomes, and how their learning influenced the levels of student achievement and what gaps still exist that require additional emphasis on their learning. It is also a time in which discoveries are made and the potential and possibilities for impact to teaching and learning structures are uncovered and shared with others. Teachers facilitate the work of changing practice with each other. They support the implementation of new practices through peer coaching and feedback. This process is grounded in individual and community improvement. Learning is in the relationships between people (Lave & Wenger, 1991).

Professional learning communities are where learners come together to problem solve and create new conditions for learning for students. Such new conditions could be new instructional strategies for challenged learning, new curriculum, revising regulations, policies to serve students, and so on. The awesome power in this process is that two or more learners (Learner–Learner) come together to construct knowledge that will impact the structures of education for years to come, as in curriculum development, or make the difference in the learning for the student who has not experienced success for years—or, sadly, never experienced success at all as a learner. No matter if the co-constructed knowledge shapes the world or shapes one child who will shape the world, the focus of two or more people learning together to change the world one student at a time is simply transformational as a process!

The good news is that PLCs provide the right environment for learners coming together. The Learner–Learner model thrives using learning communities as a conduit to bring two or more people together to co-construct meaning of their learning. However, schools are challenged with bringing learners together because the structure of schools does not provide teachers the *time* to come together. One of the most challenging factors schools face in initiating and creating learning communities is that of time. However, time is the factor that central offices, superintendents, school boards, and school-based leaders can influence. Boyd (1992) enumerated a list of physical factors needed in a context conducive to change and improvements: availability of needed resources; schedules and structures that reduce isolation; and policies that provide greater autonomy, foster collaboration, provide effective communication, and provide staff development. Louis and Kruse (1995) offer a similar list: time to meet and talk, physical proximity of the staff to one another, teaching roles that are interdependent, communication structures, school autonomy, and teacher empowerment. The bad news is that as we continue to strive to provide these structures, the hardest resource to capture of all of the above is time. However, in an virtual learning community, relational factors and human capacities have a different view. Online virtual learning communities are catalysts to avoid this isolation and address the oh-too-common challenge of time! The collaborative platforms in virtual classrooms address the communication, isolation, and collaboration.

Learning in a *virtual learning community* supports the Learner–Learner model and affords participants an opportunity to function as a learning community of professionals. The Learner–Learner model presupposes that there is a symbiotic relationship between people in a learning environment that grows out of co-construction of knowledge. This development and acquisition of knowledge is supported through the use of a virtual collaborative platform. In the virtual learning community, educators learn from the course facilitator and other educators. The course facilitator does not own all of the information but does facilitate the participants' ability to obtain it through the use of technology and the implementation of the tenets of the Learner–Learner model.

This book will identify the processes of how professional learning facilitators served as guides in a Learner–Learner environment enhanced by a virtual collaborative platform. Aspects of this transformational process of learning for teachers will be highlighted in this book. This book will identify that when using technology as a resource, participants are able to collaborate with other participants, refine their thinking, and expand their learning opportunities across the boundaries of physical proximity, which leads to higher levels of teaching quality and performance and new structures of learning to impact the world for years to come.

SECTION FIVE: THE LEARNER IS THE TEACHER IN A VIRTUAL LEARNING COMMUNITY

The first step in ensuring true change in a classroom and placing learning at the center is having a teacher who understands and values knowledge acquisition in his/her own development. This teacher should consistently reach out to other educators in her building, creating a collegial professional environment. He or she should be involved in socially constructing meaning of teaching structures with others in the school through professional learning communities, peer observations, and self-reflection. Through technology, this virtual development can occur in a network of schools across town, in another state, and in another country. However, it is equally as powerful in one school! (See Chapter 6 to learn more about virtual-learning school-based cohorts.)

Learners will use these social networking structures to pose questions to a problem-based dilemma, to view model lessons, to learn new content, and to stay abreast of the latest research and be active members in a professional learning network that includes teachers, professors, principals, and educational philosophers. If teachers are learning without boundaries, the concept can become more concrete than abstract for them, and shared learning becomes richly infused and enhanced learning. In turn, they can begin to transfer this type of learning culture by using the ideals of the Learner–Learner model with their students. Too often, after teachers leave their preservice college experiences, they forget to view themselves as learners! This publication will make strong parallels between what we now know as professional learning communities and what this author will term a virtual learning community. Because of the powerful networking tools of the 21st century, teacher preparation and learning can come in real time from many different perspectives, have various approaches, challenge teachers' thinking like never before, help pull them out of their isolated realm of learning, and open them up to full collaboration, shared decision making, collective thinking, and planning with other educators.

With virtual learning communities, the barriers and isolated events surrounding knowledge are no more! Web 2.0 places users on a two-way information highway. Information and knowledge about effective teaching and learning can be shared and received as often, and as much as the learner desires, and with a choice on how to receive it. Collaborative technology platforms such as those used in social media have empowered educators and experts to weigh in on topics that are meaningful to them and furthermore to place their issues and expertise on the front line of the educational debate. According to Learning Forward (2011), "technology facilitates and expands community interaction, learning, resource archiving and sharing, and knowledge construction and sharing" (p. 25). Virtual conferences and professional-learning networks have changed the way we look at knowledge acquisition. When these two are paired and supported by the tenets of the Learner–Learner model, you get a high-powered virtual learning community of educators who are in full control of their growth and development as effective teachers and leaders.

The more one educator's learning is shared and supported by others, the more quickly the culture of continuous improvement, collective responsibility, and high expectations for students and educators grows. Collective responsibility and participation foster peer-to-peer support for learning and maintain a consistent focus on shared goals within and across communities. (Learning Forward, 2011, p. 25)

2

Getting It Started

A Planning Guide

SECTION ONE: WHY ONLINE PROFESSIONAL DEVELOPMENT?

Our online culture grew out of a need to create high-quality learning while building capacity in support of a dwindling budget and human resources. There was also a need to provide more time for professional learning, which was being heavily conducted after school hours. However, schools could no longer use this time for professional learning because they were becoming engaged in after-school mandated activities, which took precedence over time for high-quality professional learning.

After identifying the need, there were some critical steps taken before and during the development and implementation of our virtual learning community.

With Budget Cuts...How Can We Do Anything? Have You Heard This Story Before?

The Learner–Learner model was created out of the need to build capacity for professional learning opportunities while supporting collaboration and collective learning structures. The onset of budget cuts was affecting our ability to create engaging face-to-face professional-learning sessions for district employees. The members of the department were dwindling and the need to provide support to a myriad of district priorities was growing. We were competing with local school initiatives for time to provide high-quality professional learning due to schools being mandated to provide a variety of after-school workshops in support of increasing accountability mandates. Through the review of a variety of professional-learning structures that would provide virtual learning opportunities, we started with a platform that provided online courses with no feedback, follow-up, or close alignment with district priorities. This structure met a need, but it did not provide the clear learning objectives or high-quality learning structures we had grown accustomed to in support of teaching quality. Therefore, we set out on a quest to develop a structure that would allow collective and collaborative learning, build capacity to meet the needs of district employees, and support a high-quality, sustainable professional-learning environment. It was important for us to provide a level of collaboration and simultaneous learning.

The aspects of the Learner-Learner model will be highlighted in this book. This learning design transitioned out of this need. The term is a by-product of a design that was created through trial, error, and success in our quest to support a time of transition. Our static face-to-face professional-learning offerings eventually evolved into a symbiotic, dynamic community supported through planned professional-learning structures using technology. This book will demonstrate through our planned actions that online education is not merely uploading teaching materials, receiving and sending e-mail messages, and posting discussion topics on the Internet. More importantly, it is learners learning from each other as supported and identified through social constructivism. Online professional development in a professional social network of learning provides an arena for an interactive, deep, collaborative, and multidimensional thinking and learning in an educational community. In order to get these types of results, you have to have a plan.

It is said that in education, we often jump into initiatives at the central office without considering other factors that should deter us, or we simply add something new to the plate and do not consider our overall goals. Before embarking upon this journey, you need to be able to ask some clarifying questions to keep yourself outside of this cycle. Simply stated, you need to have a plan. We all know that if you fail to plan, you plan to fail! I have provided a list of questions in the chart below that will serve as a planning guide, and following it, I have provided you with the answers that were critical for us to move forward. Once you clarify some key areas, your direction will impact policies and practices you are currently instituting and those you will develop for the future. As well, there will be great consideration for how you use your resources to start this endeavor and to sustain it. Take the questions below and meet with the team of colleagues that will utilize this tool and determine your direction based upon your collective responses. Perhaps, as you review our responses, you may find your district or school somewhere in the same place we were, and this may offer some insight to your decisions and, most importantly, your actions.

Chart 2A   10 Clarifying Questions and a Planning Guide for Implementing Online PD to Get You Started!

What are the questions to get you started?	*What are the answers to get you moving?*	*What are the resources to make it happen?*	*Who will need to be on the team to get this done?*	*What action has been taken to accomplish your goal of online PD?*
Question 1: How will you align online PD with school and/ or district priorities?				
Question 2: How will you align your budget to support online PD? How will your budget support the transition from only face-to-face courses to an online community?				
Question 3: Can you partner with the instructional technology department, or do you have someone on staff who is knowledgeable in this area?				

Chart 2A   Continued

What are the questions to get you started?	What are the answers to get you moving?	What are the resources to make it happen?	Who will need to be on the team to get this done?	What action has been taken to accomplish your goal of online PD?
Question 4: How can you market this new way of learning to end users? Why would they choose this format over previous formats for learning?				
Question 5: What training will you provide to your internal course developers or subject matter experts as well as your technology support?				
Question 6: How will you capture staff development or continuing education units?				

(Continued)

Chart 2A   Continued

What are the questions to get you started?	What are the answers to get you moving?	What are the resources to make it happen?	Who will need to be on the team to get this done?	What action has been taken to accomplish your goal of online PD?
Question 7: How will you compensate online instructors? How can you capture the hours of instruction?				
Question 8: What instructional design methods will you use to deliver class content?				
Question 9: How will you measure impact of the structure? How will you evaluate learning?				
Question 10: How will you select a platform or a learning-management system to support this structure of learning? What are some platform examples that you are familiar with?				

3

10 Action Steps to Virtual Learning Communites

Action One: Align Online Professional Development (PD) With Other District/School Priorities for PD

We are far too busy and have too few resources to reinvent the wheel! This process of using an online platform for learning and dissemination of information is to support your process of talent management as well as training and development for those you support in your district. Before you start out on this journey, determine how the district's or school's other priorities can be enhanced or facilitated through this process. It may be beneficial to start by just brainstorming all the programs and initiatives you have going, examining how they are being facilitated, and considering if this option would allow you to still get the job done or, again, enhance and improve the process. On many levels, district- and school-based priorities can be accomplished through an interactive platform that allows participants to gain knowledge and pose new questions for clarification. We currently use e-mail systems as well as other electronic means to do this. Many of these systems are asynchronous and don't allow for an opportunity to interact with other participants. Some quick examples of common practices that all districts and schools use are board policies. In addition, information concerning instruction and curriculum as well as technology and human resources concerns can be distributed through a virtual learning platform.

Most districts' and schools' overarching goal is to ensure that every teacher is prepared to meet school, district, state, and federal guidelines as they relate to student achievement outcomes. This is what is expected from all schools and school systems. However, our unique challenge has always been determining structures through which we can touch every teacher without compromising the fidelity of the training, differentiating the needs for novice and seasoned teachers, and providing adequate funding so that all teachers receive the benefit from the training. Since we are so large and have many employees, online professional development has become a very viable option. This structure allows us to ensure consistent delivery of content, differentiate to the needs of the personnel, and ensure that the appropriate personnel receive pertinent information in support of their positions.

Some examples of how we meet a variety of district needs through this format are online courses on school and district budget process, evaluating teachers and other personnel, and navigating the IEP process for current and new teachers. The list also includes ways we have used this collaborative process of customizing courses to meet a variety of district priorities and needs. Each of these areas was born out of a problem. The virtual learning community allowed learners to come together, collectively address the problems, determine shared solutions, and gain a greater understanding of the concepts shared by the facilitator and among members of the group. Whether your challenge is size or, as it is for many schools, just lack of time and an isolated culture, a platform for virtual online learning can provide real-time information that is quick, accessible, and differentiated to meet a variety of needs.

Anything that becomes a part of the fabric of the local school should include a good plan for implementation and purpose with support from those in leadership roles. Each one of these critical components must be active for the school to adopt this learning as part of the fabric of learning at that local school.

Action Two: Write the Integration of Your Online Platform Into the Budget. It Is the Answer to Reduction in Resources

Human and financial resources are being decreased due to budget cuts. However, the need for teachers and the priority of creating effective teachers have increased. *The supply has dwindled, but the demand has increased.* Perhaps for the first few months of budget cuts, you are paralyzed and feel overwhelmed with expectations. I can relate to this feeling; this was my exact initial experience. However, the needs did not go away, and I had a job to do for the benefit of the teachers and the students. After a while, we realized that we had to determine a solution to this clear, consistent, and necessary priority. Since our staff could not provide in-depth, one-on-one support for more than 100 schools and 13,000 employees, online professional development was viewed as a realistic way to provide high-quality support.

By providing each school with a dedicated virtual learning space through a platform and training external and internal staff on the effective use of the tools in the online platform, schools can create learning opportunities for their teachers that support their priorities and needs as well as engage in those that are created by the district. *Where we were paying for materials, reimbursement to district staff for travel, hard copies of books, and the cost of time, this option provided all schools the same resources with an opportunity to customize to meet their individual needs, which was not a viable option in the previous model.* All materials and resources are loaded in on online platform. In addition, the teachers have an opportunity to see the strategy they are learning about in action through high-quality videos as well as have a reflective conversation with other colleagues in the school or outside of the school in support of differentiated and individualized learning. District courses were being offered online, and the facilitators did not have to use budgeted funds to purchase materials, use building space, or be reimbursed for travel to the schools. In addition, developing structures within the virtual space with assistance from the department of professional learning is a viable option to meet many district priorities that focus on the management aspect for leaders such as budgeting, evaluation, policies, and so forth. This structure supports a continuous collaborative relationship between the local school and professional learning (PL) department to support faculty and staff and create continuous learning experiences that are unique to the local school and support district priorities.

ACTION THREE: TRANSITION YOUR FACE-TO-FACE COMMUNITY OF LEARNERS TO AN ONLINE COMMUNITY

Developing or instituting a training process for online facilitators is critical to the success of your online courses. Teaching a face-to-face course is very different than being an online facilitator. Once your facilitators understand the tools required in an online platform to engage the learner, the tenets of professional learning communities can be applied in the online setting. We created a policy and a practice that certifies instructors as online facilitators. This training is offered to all who are interested a few times a year. This has allowed us to build capacity and create a sustainable process. Without proper training and development of the facilitators, the quality of the online community and courses would suffer.

Online content can be redesigned from face-to-face content. Courses that have been previously developed by content experts in the district provide the best foundation for getting started. However, not all content experts have the technical knowledge or desire to create online courses. It is necessary to provide content experts training on the platform as well as online teaching strategies based upon their interest in offering their courses in this format. The internal developers can offer this training. As well, it proved to be beneficial for us to pair content experts, also known as subject matter experts, and online course developers. Ideally, the expert who developed the course content would facilitate the course. But some experts will not have the knowledge or desire to facilitate an online course. In those cases, facilitators are trained on the course content.

ACTION FOUR: PARTNER WITH THE INSTRUCTIONAL TECHNOLOGY GURUS IN YOUR DISTRICT OR SCHOOL

If your district has an instructional technology division, you can generally transfer the structure being used to design lessons for students to meet the needs of your teachers/educators. Having a person on board who has done this will help you reach your goal. It will be necessary to partner with the instructional technology division or provide instructional technology design training for a current employee who can serve as your technical resource guide for this project. In our district, when an opening was vacant, my goal was to hire someone with the skills of an instructional technology expert and a teacher. Once that person was hired, it was my job to provide training on aspects of high-quality professional learning to this staff member. This employee has successfully merged these two worlds and has trained more than 50 employees as certified facilitators of online professional learning. The facilitators continue to function in their roles as teachers, administrators, and district personnel. Our structure affords them an opportunity to serve as facilitators off contract time.

Technical resources are as good as what is provided by the school district. A few areas can be assessed for technical resources such as participant access: what type of access do your participants have at school, at home, in a professional learning room, and so on? Human resources are probably harder to come by than the technical resources. You need personnel who aren't afraid to allow the technology to guide the learning and be in the forefront of the knowledge cycle. You want this person to have a good understanding of Web-based resources. You will need someone who has a desire and interest to galvanize resources under a clear vision for learning. The technology resources typically used for student engagement in technology-centric learning environments transfer easily to adult learning environments. These resources, coupled with professional learning standards, are the cornerstones to the implementation of a virtual learning community.

ACTION FIVE: MARKET TO THE END USERS—ENGAGE THEM IN THE PROCESS

Technology use has increased over the past several years in all arenas, but education is still moving slowly. We were aware that there was a demand for this type of professional development, but this demand was not communicated by the majority of our teachers. We started small and offered a few classes that were interest-based professional learning instead of need based. Some of these courses are listed in Chapter 4. We also originally designed the courses with very few collaborative tools such as discussion areas, chat rooms, webinars, and other synchronous (real-time) and asynchronous (response at any time) forms of collaboration. The orginal forums allowed the end users to focus only on content and not on a new process. This was done to transition the learners into this new format of learning. We were excited to have them sign in online and complete a course that was in a new format for them. At the onset, we offered opportunities for them to provide reflective feedback on this process and add ideas to the overall design of these courses. We also transitioned through stages of concern with very focused steps (see Chart 3A). Two years later, we have increased our courses exponentially, and we have instituted a district-based required training for facilitators who use online professional learning. All of our teachers and hundreds of other district staff have used the online virtual learning community platform. Our requests for face-to-face learning are decreasing, and the demand for virtual learning community classes increases each semester. We have also infused all of our courses with collaborative tools and created an active and engaging learning platform, leading to the virtual learning community.

A few department members welcomed the shift initially, but many had more questions than faith in the process before it started: How will we know they are learning? What if they are uncomfortable with online learning? How will we monitor? It was important to determine the answer so that we could have a full commitment from our developers. Once we muddled through the initial stages of this being a new way of learning, we began to see a level of excitement and full engagement from those that really wanted to be part of something innovative. Without a doubt, it was important to have a marketing campaign that included training, implementation procedures, communication, and a process for feedback of any concerns.

How Did We Address the Resistant and Reluctant Learners?

It was important for us to understand the unmet needs, concerns, and fears of our learners. As shared in Knowles's (1973) andragogic model of adult learning, the learning environment must be collaborative. Because we chose to start with hybrid or blended models for our initial classes, all participants started the class in the traditional face-to-face format. It was during this initial session, which was generally less than an hour, that norms and the process for this type of learning were established and participants were given an opportunity to provide feedback and express any fear to the facilitator prior to transitioning to the online virtual learning community. Goals were expressed and the design of the class was mutually determined by the participants and facilitator in support of the Learner–Learner structure of learning. Though the participants rarely made any requests for the instructor to modify the design, the commitment was that they were provided the opportunity to express concerns if they desired. This initial face-to-face session also supported an active culture of learning once the participants were engaged in the virtual learning community. They had an established relationship with the facilitator and other learners in the class, which supported them with reflections as well as feedback to the facilitator and other learners.

However, before the implementation of the class, it was important for me to provide opportunities for our learners to communicate concerns regarding the implementation of this new method of providing professional learning. The Concerns-Based Adoption Model (CBAM) identifies seven stages of concern that people go through during a new project or initiative (Hord, Rutherford, Hullin-Auston, & Hall, 1987). This model contends that concerns are associated with unmet needs, and unmet needs cause individuals or groups to become resistant to new ideas. Please note the stages below and the strategies we used to address these needs in Chart 3A.

Chart 3A   Concerns-Based Adoption Stages—Strategies Used to Address Need

Stage of Concern	Unmet Need	Strategy Used to Address Unmet Need
Awareness	Group members were unaware that something new was coming.	We provided flyers in the professional development brochure a semester prior to implementation. Also informed participants that it would not replace face-to-face classes.
Informational	Group members needed specific Information about the new Idea and how it would be implemented.	The flyer detailed the new methods of learning—termed the *PLeCampus*—with a full description and examples of classes that would be offered, detailing the format of virtual learning communities.
Personal	Group members were not aware of how the new program would affect them.	Each school has a professional learning liaison. This teacher leader provided detailed information about the virtual learning communities and was available to answer questions.

Chart 3A   Continued

Stage of Concern	Unmet Need	Strategy Used to Address Unmet Need
Management	Group members had management concerns related to time, materials, and coordination.	The virtual learning community classes would be offered by the district as a support to all personnel. The district started this process by answering the leading questions provided in Step 1. Information to highlight how this format would save teachers time and the need to have materials was provided.
Consequences	Group members questioned the benefit to students and whether it would be worth the effort.	The benefit to students was tied to the participants' engagement in the learning process of evaluating their new skills and practices during and after the class. This was discussed in the initial face-to-face session.
Collaboration	Group members had concerns related to working together.	The Learner–Learner model fully supports collaboration in virtual learning communities. It is always highlighted in the communication.
Refocusing	The new program had been implemented; the group members were interested in the next new phase to be added.	Throughout the implementation, group members were provided opportunities to give formal feedback. In addition, a focus group was established in support of the next phase of implementation.

Adapted from Hall & Hord (1987).

Action Six: Train Your Subject Matter Experts—Grow Your Own Facilitators

As mentioned previously, it will be beneficial to partner with your technology department or a *technology guru*. It will be necessary to have someone on staff that is knowledgeable about instructional technology or to partner with the department that facilitates technology in your district. In order to build capacity, it will be critical for this person to train and develop others.

Because of the size of our district, we trained and identified a few internal developers who are go-to people for our online professional development structure. We also developed virtual professional learning coaches that serve to support schools and teachers with technical questions and troubleshooting. See Chapter 6 for more information on virtual professional learning coaches.

Training the internal developers and facilitators is critical. The process is not arduous, but in order to support consistency, this action step cannot be omitted. This process should occur before there are online courses offered to end users. Usually the training will involve development on instructional technology design processes and effective online facilitation strategies. In addition, training is done on the chosen platform so that the internal developers are comfortable with navigating the aspects that are provided or can request additional aspects that may be needed from the online platform partner.

Teaching a face-to-face course is very different than being an online facilitator. Once your facilitators understand the tools required in an online platform to engage the learner, the tenets of learning communities can be applied in the online setting. We have created a policy and a practice that certifies instructors as online facilitators. This has allowed us to build capacity and created a sustainable process. Without proper training and development of the facilitators, the quality of the online community and courses would suffer.

In order to accomplish this task, we offer a course created by our online course designer a few times a year (see Chapter 6 for the course outline). It is our goal to have many online facilitators trained. The course is offered to any district employee who is interested. We believe that even if those who take the course never get an opportunity to facilitate a course with adults, these skills and strategies can be transferred to classrooms with students. Because we are such a large district, we truly believe in learning bundling. Some people refer to this as "train the trainer." It is our belief that when our teacher and district leaders are trained in a new concept, they, by nature of the design of education organizations, have the capability of transferring this skill to others in formal and informal structures, which provides opportunities for us to bundle the learning. It also supports sustainability of instructional strategies that support student learning.

All developers who were subject matter experts were immersed in an online course in which they participated in intense training that supported their level of proficiency and provided the perfect arena for our first cohort of virtual learning community members. The facilitators were engaged in the practices they would eventually facilitate for end users, such as ongoing reflective discussions in the platform, various levels of virtual interactions that were synchronous and asynchronous, and communication using Web 2.0 tools that contain audio and video capability, as well as creating modules that include all of these components before completing the course. They studied the theory of social constructivist learning and adult learning theory first and foremost before creating professional-learning modules. Once they were certified in this course, which fully prepares them for one-to-one instruction or any online professional learning, they submitted proposals to design and teach courses. The courses were reviewed and feedback was provided when necessary. If approved, they signed the policy statement, designed their courses in the platform, and they were advertised in our district published catalog of courses with all other courses offered in the district.

The online facilitator course was a good example of the Learner–Learner model. The course is designed so that the facilitators learn from the content in the course and each other as they engage in the course. As new facilitators are trained to become online facilitators, they reach out to those already trained and ask us questions or share their experiences.

It is extremely important that subject matter experts are trained in online pedagogy. We want to maintain the integrity of any content that is being taught and partner it with good online design. In collaboration with many departments across the district, we have partnered with departments such as special education, curriculum and instruction, and human resources to provide the richest content available through an engaging online platform.

Through course development, we wanted to ensure ownership; a majority of the courses are facilitated by those who developed them. This ensures that the person facilitating the course understands and is familiar with the content being presented. However, we also use the model in which our online developer has structured some courses that are facilitated by our cadre of online facilitators.

ACTION SEVEN: OFFER INCENTIVES: GIVE YOUR END USERS STAFF DEVELOPMENT CREDITS AND COMPENSATE YOUR ONLINE FACILITATORS

Online course facilitators are required to monitor the number of hours participants are logged in to the platform. In addition, they are expected to provide an outline of their course to the department through an approval process, specifying the number of hours it will take to complete each activity. When advertising their course, these requirements are communicated. The platform we use calculates time spent in the online community and provides the district leaders a report for each participant in each class. The instructor has to provide this documentation at the end of each course before a participant is given credit. In addition, the instructor has to sign an agreement regarding this expected practice. When choosing an online platform, it will be necessary to determine how hours of use are calculated and how this will be reported within the online platform.

It is my belief that our online facilitators would do this work even if they were not getting paid. The majority of the online facilitators are dedicated master teachers who have strategies to share. However, with the shift in resources, we were able to provide compensation for their hours of online instruction, which is mostly done during off-contract hours. We do have district staff who provide learning during contract hours and offer courses in which they support schools during the day. Online facilitators are compensated based upon the number of professional learning/staff development units assigned to the course. They follow specific guidelines for calculating the number of hours the participants will spend on this course, which is aligned to their credit. An instructor's number of contact hours can vary for a course depending on the technical level and/or experience with online learning offered by each participant. The current method of aligning the number of hours to the number of staff development units has proven to be the most consistent and fair method.

All online facilitators are compensated with $35.00 an hour, and every 10-hour course equals one staff development unit (SDU) for the participants. Each course with compensation is offered in 10-hour increments. Online facilitators are required to meet the class in a virtual asynchronous classroom, which constitutes course hours. We developed a policy in which compensation as well as required hours of instruction are clearly outlined. This policy statement also includes some basic expectations of course development and required communication and feedback to participants for high levels of engagement. Instructors are only compensated for off-contract hours of work.

ACTION EIGHT: DESIGN YOUR COURSES TO MEET THE NEEDS OF YOUR END USERS

The design model we have instituted was a process and an evolution for us as we planned and created professional learning opportunities for adults. I composed the Learner–Learner model as this structure of learning became a clear reality for us as a district, and we were able to conceptualize as well as implement a structure that provided the impact we were seeking for our adult learners. This model is based on the premise of social constructivist theory. The learners in a course are expected to learn in a social environment, create meaning, and gain new knowledge from their experiences through each other. The virtual learning community can only be instituted when the aspects of the Learner-Learner model are apparent. When instructors design courses, they must embed the aspects of this model in the course design.

Initially, we were most concerned with use, and specifically ease of use, of our online courses. We did not consistently provide the feedback loop through discussion or the process of sharing strategies. It was primarily a space in which we provided content on instructional strategies. Many of the resources were uploaded as PDF files or PowerPoints and access to videos. Though this information was useful and valuable, it did not provide for the reflection that is required in a professional learning community. As we gained feedback from our users, we noticed that the opportunity for them to learn from each other was one of the cornerstones to high levels of engagement. Not only did they need to learn from each other, but we also needed to provide tools that supported collaboration and collective opportunities for them to learn from each other. We started off with courses that were of interest to teachers as well as those designed by our platform developer. Once we had a consistent group of users, we began to identify specific courses that supported the data of our district as well as integrated Web 2.0 tools to support engagement. We collaborated with subject matter experts and paired them with online developers/facilitators. From there, we instituted a full-district rollout of high-yield strategies, which was offered to all teachers, instructional coaches, and administrators. District and school needs should drive the criteria for selecting courses. However, course design should take teachers from the 20th century into the 21st century, such as exposure to Web 2.0 components, blogging, social media, iPad/iPod applications, and the like. This process has been a transition for our district, and we are most recently, through our virtual learning communities, embarking upon this territory. There is work yet to be done to fully integrate all of our online courses using these tools, but the cornerstones of our design are embedded in technology-centric and collaborative learning structures.

ACTION NINE: MEASURE THE IMPACT OF THE LEARNING STRUCTURE ON TEACHER PRACTICES

Evaluating the impact of the use of online professional development courses on teacher practices and student achievment continues to be a challenge. We are proficient when it comes to determining the affective and behavioral components of our courses. We know our teachers like online learning, and they incorporate strategies that they have learned in their classroom settings. However, we are not as sure how to effectively answer the question regarding the impact their newfound practices have on student achievement. We have determined based on feedback from our teacher users that students are more engaged and can assume that their new learning using the online format has positively impacted student learning. But we do not have a system in place to determine student achievement. This area continues to be one of great need and focus.

Just as you do in a good face-to-face course, you must provide some time for the participants to (1) interact with one another and (2) reflect or complete an activity to reinforce their learning. One lesson learned is that people do not learn as much when there is no work for them to do. The "work" can include discussions, journaling, completing a check sheet, watching a video and reflecting on it, or focusing on a project they will implement in their classroom or work environment, but it is critical for them to engage in learning by doing.

ACTION TEN: DETERMINE AN ONLINE DELIVERY PLATFORM

Part of the journey into considering an online platform was guided by my commitment to the Learner-Learner model. We needed more than online videos that captured teacher practices or PDF files that were created by the platform developer that were designed for schools and communities all over this nation. We needed more than an opportunity for an administrator to find an online lesson in support of a particular area of need and send that link to the teacher with a few reflective questions. We needed an opportunity for the teachers to reflect on their learning in a professional community guided by a content expert and a person who was knowledgeable and proficient in adult learning strategies. We needed a platform that would allow us to take online videos and customize those strategies to reflective questions, ongoing dialogue, and opportunities for practice in between with immediate feedback. We needed a platform that would support Web 2.0 tools so that learning would be symbiotic between the facilitator and participants and, most of all, engaging for the learners. However, we met with many providers and have selected platforms that meet our needs and supports the Learner–Learner model. Platform providers should be viable and wonderful partners in this work and extend opportunities through constant and consistent dialogue. They should be very responsive to district and school goals and continue to expand their opportunities as they learn about your needs. This collaboration supports the Learner–Learner model of collaboration. As you determine a partner, having an open relationship in which design discussions are addressed and considered is paramount to your success.

I continue to search for a course platform that contains all of the learning applications to support the Learner–Learner environment. This platform will inherently allow for critical thinking on case studies and be able to merge components of learning and allow for critical collective questioning on the part of the instructor and each learner, along with personalized and enhanced learning tied directly to student performance. To visualize this environment, this platform will allow us to pass the learning around so that it is never static. It is an environment in which each participant is an active and engaged member, adding to the body of work that is created through collaborative structures of learning. This platform will give users an opportunity to automatically connect in a synchronous environment at any time of the day in any location. This platform will provide a structure through which teachers can tag the practices they learned and have co-constructed with the facilitator other participants with specific student performance in their classrooms in an environment in which the community can view these new skills and the examples of enhanced student performance. In this platform, teachers will continue to develop their new ideas using discussion format, wikis, chat rooms, and shared files to build upon the community's shared knowledge. We currently use technology tools that allow for some of this shared and collective learning, but these structures are not inherently built into a platform. Everything about the platform should convey learning and support open-ended critical thinking with an automatic, built-in portfolio of documented learning that participants can take from the course and use to build on their body of knowledge as they engage in future courses. What this looks like in practice is a virtual learning community with inherent and intuitive structures of communication through which the participants in this community are able to share ideas back and forth in synchronous and asynchronous platforms with all group members, including the facilitator. It is imperative that during learning, the learners should be able to record "aha" moments as the learning is happening and be able to provide immediate feedback to the other learners in the community. This is what happens in a face-to-face professional learning community. The premise of the structure is always about *the learning of the learners*. A professional learning community is professionals who come to together and focus on their learning. We have demonstrated that this can be done in an online environment. We have had to provide structures as highlighted above to support this process. So a perfect platform will have all of these structure included.

In the end, we want our participants to have the ability to engage in this type of learning community, eventually tie their learning back to their facilitation of learning with students, and be able to demonstrate through evaluation how their learning impacted the performance and learning of those students. As you search for a platform, let the tenets of a professional learning community and the Learner-Learner model guide your actions.

4

The Process

Transitioning a Face-to-Face Professional Learning Community to an Online Virtual Learning Community

Online instruction provided an opportunity for us to offer instruction using technology as the medium. Online delivery provided an opportunity to extend human resources and time by distributing learning using the Internet. There were some unforeseeable challenges that were met when our district had to decrease the number of employees. We were offering more than 100 face-to-face classes from a menu of options to schools through participant selection. For the past 15 to 20 years, the department published a catalog. The courses in this catalog were determined by district needs based upon student data and employee interest. These courses were available to any district employee and focused on a range of topics that were academically related, such as Differentiation in Math, Guided Reading Strategies, and How to Teach Fluency, as well as personal-skill related such as Anger Management, Time Management, and Team Building. We offered these classes on site at the district office or at various school sites in the district. They were offered after school hours from 4:00 p.m. to 8:00 p.m. and would be offered in 10-, 20-, 30-, 40-, and 50-hour increments. Generally, the participants would have to attend at least two to three evenings that were often stretched over a few weeks. There was a period when these classes were at capacity with 25 to 30 participants. We had often had a waiting list for several of them. In 2008, we began to see this trend diminish. We were able to determine that one of the major factors impacting the decline of enrollment was time participants had to add this to their already-full plates. The time participants had previously had to attend these classes was diminishing as school-based accountability structures increased. Therefore, online professional development became a very viable option for our district. It supported many features, which are discussed in the following sections.

SECTION ONE: ONLINE AND BLENDED LEARNING OPPORTUNITIES PROVIDED OUR TEACHERS AN ALTERNATIVE TO THE TRADITIONAL PROFESSIONAL LEARNING EXPERIENCE

The blended model is vital to the transfer from face-to-face to online. The blended model affords the facilitator an opportunity to ensure that the participants are not only comfortable but also competent enough to participate and navigate through the online professional learning communities. Blended courses also meet the needs of those learners who are not quite ready for 100% online instruction and are still in need of the comfort of a face-to-face facilitator. Another alternative to the blended course are webinars; our webinar courses bring instruction to the comfort of home or classroom after hours. Participants are given a time to log on and participate in the course with the facilitator and other classmates via the computer. Both of these sources allow participants a vehicle through which to transition to online learning.

Some participants felt more connected when they could meet the instructor, so we provided alternatives. Providing a transitional method, such as a blended model, is an excellent means to transition from the traditional face-to-face method of providing professional learning to the online method. Providing this format to teachers and administrators creates an opportunity for learning and the implementation of new skills in the delivery of professional learning and the development of diverse learning communities.

In addition, online learning supported the demanding schedule and conflict of time required for site-based expectations of the teachers. They were able to go home after a long day of work, address personal needs, and pick back up with learning with a clearer focus on improving their craft. The 24-hour access provided this flexibility of their time. In addition, they were not rushed with trying to meet at a designated time in a face-to-face class.

The number of participants has steadily and gradually grown. Word of mouth and the excitement for this alternative are helping the program to grow. As time progresses, online PD is becoming a part of the way we do PD in our district.

SECTION TWO: COMMUNICATION VIA THE COMPUTER AND THE WEB PROVIDED 24-HOUR ACCESS

Infrastructure for technology access 24 hours a day is a major consideration when offering online professional development. It is beneficial to provide this opportunity. As we transition as a nation to upgrading our infrastructure in support of technology, we are still faced with school campuses on which there is no or limited and inconsistent access to technology. The ability to offer courses through the Web provided our learners with access to the course content when they were at home or even if they were out of town. Participants were also able to access sites that were blocked at the district such as YouTube, which is a great tool for engaging the adult learner and accessing learning material.

As well, the benefits of providing 24-hour access via the Web as a means of providing professional learning are important for facilitators. They no longer need to worry about tardiness and absences from a course or limited access due to location and time of the course. Twenty-four-hour access online allows participants to meet deadlines and complete assignments at their own leisure. It also supports collaboration any time participants can access chat rooms, participate in webinar sessions, and engage in class discussions from the comfort of their chosen learning environment.

The 24-hour access has been a big bonus of our online PD courses. Almost all participants will tell you that they were able to fit the course into their busy schedules in ways that were convenient for them. Twenty-four-hour access is one of the reasons that some of our participants even try the online course.

Section Three: The Methods Used to Deliver Online Courses Provide a Level of Professional Learning Differentiation to Participants

We were certain that providing online professional learning through only PowerPoint presentations and PDF files would eventually become monotonous and create disengagement and disinterest from our users. Therefore, it was important for our facilitators to receive training on Web 2.0 tools as options to incorporate into their course designs. Some of the Web 2.0 tools incorporated by facilitators were the use of a wiki space for individualized concept development and demonstration of participants' work in their classrooms; integration of a Prezi to create engagement for presentations when sharing content and co-construction of new ideas; Edmodo, which provided the teachers an additional level of social collaboration and gave them a tool to use with their students; bubbl.us for online brainstorming; Poll Everywhere, which can be used with mobile devices and is often used in the hybrid model for the initial face-to-face course to ascertain information from the participants regarding their use of online PD or specific topics of learning; Google Docs to support the sharing of documents among community members; Storybird, which many of the teachers began to use with students in their classrooms after using it in the learning community as a unique method to document their learning; podcasts as a unique method to share and highlight their own personal journey of learning through voice for the others in their community; and YouTube, which is a great visual method for demonstrating the concepts that participants are learning. The goal is to appeal to adult learning strategies, differentiate the learning for our users, and fully engage their minds so that they are not feeling like they are staring at a computer screen with no interaction or involvement. Web 2.0 tools provide a variety of interactive experiences.

The facilitators had a hard time transitioning from using PowerPoint because as teachers, which most of our facilitators are, they were accustomed to using that tool in their classrooms. However, as learners and observers of learning, they understood the need to transition because the end users provided feedback. They also realized, when using the eye of a learner, that this format, used on a consistent basis, would not engage the learner, no matter how many graphics and animations the slideshows contained. Therefore, they integrated Web 2.0 tools, videos, and webinars to enhance the level of engagement in their learning communities.

In addition, the online delivery method is an excellent means of differentiating instruction for participants. Through the online virtual professional learning communities, the facilitator is able to meet a variety of learning styles. We often forget that adults have a variety of learning styles. For the needs of the visual learner who learns best with the use of pictures, diagrams, and other visual displays, the facilitator is able to provide sessions that incorporate graphics and video clips. Needs of participants who learn best through lectures and discussions are met by also providing webinar sessions and recorded chat sessions and downloading taped lectures and audiobooks. Kinesthetic learners' needs are met through the sheer navigation of the computer, the participation in virtual classrooms, and the ability to independently conduct online research.

Other methods facilitators use to differentiate the learning for adults include using time creatively. They are able to extend the time of the course for participants who find they are unable to complete course requirements in an allotted period. In face-to-face courses, participants are often required to learn the content during the time the course is offered. However, in online courses, those adjustments to time (self-directed as well as offered by the facilitator) help make the course more personalized for the participants. This extended use of time affords the learners opportunities to go deeper into assignments if needed or spend less time on content in which they may be proficient and navigate to other modules in the course to support their learning. In addition, they are asked to create examples to support and demonstrate their learning, such as videos and brochures that they can use in their current roles, and through collective collaboration, they are able to also learn from materials such as Prezis, podcasts, stories, journal entries, and Google Docs that are virtually shared by other participants in the course.

Most participants who complete the courses are very appreciative of being able to take the course online. This structure is our biggest way of differentiating learning. In reviews of our reflective assessment process, almost every teacher mentions the love of being able to work on the course whenever it is convenient for them. Several teachers mention the time factor—they are busy at school, in school, have families, and so forth and cannot take the time to travel to a location after school to take a course. In these economic times, several participants always mention being able to save gas as a huge bonus!

SECTION FOUR: THE SOCIAL DYNAMIC OF THE LEARNING ENVIRONMENT IN SUPPORT OF VIRTUAL LEARNING COMMUNITIES EXTENDS THE WALLS OF A SCHOOL TO THE DISTRICT AND OUTSIDE THE DISTRICT

In virtual learning communities (VLCs), the participants are able to socially construct information through the process of sharing. They exchange ideas and bounce strategies off each other and give each other suggestions on how to incorporate these ideas into their own courses.

Our online classes are designed to promote the concept of learning communities. All participants, including the facilitator, post a profile providing a short biography. Participants also participate in weekly discussion, where they are responsible for responding to a topic and commenting on other participants' responses. All participants must post their final project in a community area to share with their classmates. In some instances, this is done during modules on an ongoing basis. This allows participants to share their ideas and educators to build an educational resource toolbox that supports their personalized learning goals. This format of collective communication opens the doors for networking across the district and, in some instances, outside the district, as we have participants from other school systems participate in our district's professional learning online courses.

In addition, we learned early on the importance of the discussions. We build the courses so that the process is learn, discuss, learn, discuss. This level of interaction allows the facilitator and the participants to develop that symbiotic relationship with each other and form networks and partnerships that extend beyond the course. Because everyone participates and responds, even those who would normally not speak up in a face-to-face course, there is rich dialogue and discussion in a professional community of learners.

The online course format provides an opportunity for the participants to create products, post them, and gain feedback on their hard work from the other learners in the course (both the participants and the facilitator). This is the power of the co-construction of knowledge in the virtual learning community! They are able to go outside of the course environment and learn content through online tools such as YouTube, Google Docs, and other Web 2.0 tools. In addition, the course facilitator provides links to other professional networks of teachers in the nation and other sites that support the same content and instructional strategy they are studying. Embedded in the courses are links that support the learning for that VLC and continue to grow our community of learners through social aspects of learning. The online community supports our ability to offer these engaging courses to more participants online because space and resources such as paper, notebooks, books, and so forth are never a funding consideration, and the online facilitator can offer several sessions of the same course at the same time. We generally limit our communities to 25 participants to maintain the integrity of collective collaboration. Our communities and the social impact of this type of learning continue to grow because teachers are recommending courses to other teachers.

The virtual online learning community is also a perfect solution for school-based professional development. Because there can be both synchronous and asynchronous learning, online PD is very versatile and is customized to differentiate the learning needs of different types of learners, groups of teachers, grade levels, and school communities based upon their data.

Mrs. Ogletree's Discussion Board Thread Example

Please note below an example of a thread of discussion from one of the courses designed by Mrs. Ogletree, a member of the department and one of our primary trained facilitators.

The discussion was focused on formative assessments. You will see that through this discussion, other strategies were offered to the teachers. Discussion and reflection support collective ideas as well as a format for collaboration among teachers in the VLC. It also serves as an arena for guided suggestions by the instructor as the teachers apply new strategies learned in the class. Oftentimes in a face-to-face class, the session ends and the teachers have lingering questions that they do not have an opportunity to ask each other or the facilitator. In a VLC, the learning can continue, and it is also recorded and collected through discussion threads. Depending upon the type of online learning platform you use as a district or school, the participants are able to continue to participate in the social community and continue to engage in discussions with others in the course even after it has ended.

Figure 4A

Discussion Week 2   Reply to topic

Tanya Ogletree

Posted: Tue Feb 15 2011 12:33 PM

What information for this weeks lecture was most helpful to you as it relates to Formative Assessments? Why? **Please respond to at least one class participant.**

 Reply

Student One

Re: Discussion Week 2
Posted: Tue Feb 15 2011 09:53 PM

The specific strategies used to give feedback to people was the most helpful to me as it relates to Formative Assessments. The graphic organizer gave very good examples of ways to assess and provide information. By reading this organizer, I came to realize that not only does the assessment help the children, but it causes the teacher to be focused and more specific on what needs to be taught **and** how it will be taught. If you provide students with what is expected of them, then you must make sure you have taught the things to help the students reach that goal. I finally liked the question that formative assessments ask, "What do I do next?" for teachers and students. If students do well on the formative assessment provided, then what? But, what happens if they do not do so well on the assessment? This question helps drive the path of the instruction provided.

 Reply

Student Two

Re: Discussion Week 2
Posted: Thu Feb 17 2011 08:56 AM

I liked the visual of the Four Steps of the Learning Process. And the Essential Questions were very helpful.

 Reply

Student Three

Re: Re: Discussion Week 2
Posted: Mon Feb 21 2011 12:02 PM

Hello, I do Agree with you on how the Formative Assessment will help students stay on track with not only their lessons but also the goals that were set up for them by the teacher. I feel that frequent conferences with the students to let them know how they can improve their class work and master the skills that are being taught to them. They can also at the time of the conference between teacher and students ask any questions they may have for the weeks work and what they can do next to be successful.

 Reply

(Continued)

Figure 4A Continued

Student Three

Re: Re: Re: Discussion Week 2
Posted: Tue Feb 22 2011 08:30 PM

Thanks for your comments. I don't always have the time to conference with my students on an individual basis, so what I have come to do, especially with homework, and sometimes class work, is write comments on their paper. I will then gather students who I have noticed a pattern with and conference together, explaining the comments made on their papers, and asking **how** they came up with their answers. This has worked well with my class. I try to have a quick turn around as far as homework and class work assignments so they are not so far removed from it.

Reply

Tanya Ogletree

Re: Re: Discussion Week 2
Posted: Wed Feb 23 2011 09:43 PM

Hello,

I see that you like graphic organizers and a source for formative assessments. If you enjoy using graphic organizers, you will really love using thinking maps. Unlike graphic organizers, thinking maps are eight maps that correspond with fundamental thinking processes. Often times training maps are thought to be graphic organizers, but there is a very distinct difference.

Graphic Organizer or Thinking Map? What's the Difference?

A graphic organizer is used to organize thinking by giving students a pre-designed model to fill in information.

A Thinking Map is designed to help students organize their own thinking by letting them decide on the structure that best organizes the information.

When to Use a Graphic Organizer	When to Use a Thinking Map
• when you don't have time to focus on active student thinking -- you simply want them to copy and fill in information	• when you want to emphasize the student's ownership of the thinking process (they design, not just fill in)
• when you want to collapse a complicated thinking process into a single organizer	• when you want to do in-depth work rather than just pre-fabricated cutting and pasting
• when you want to provide a structure for students who have difficulty with the material (may be useful for some special education students)	• when you intend to use multiple maps to extend student thinking and as a vehicle for a larger project (a writing activity, for example)

If there is an opportunity for you or your school to participate in a Thinking Map Training please do so, you will truly be pleased.

 Reply

Figure 4A   Continued

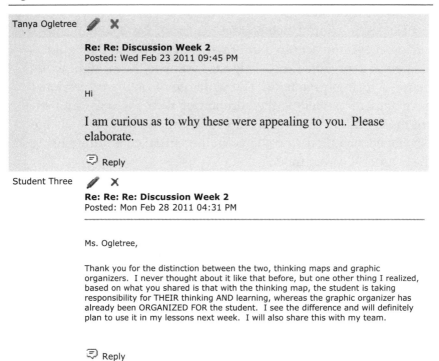

Tanya Ogletree

Re: Re: Discussion Week 2
Posted: Wed Feb 23 2011 09:45 PM

Hi

I am curious as to why these were appealing to you. Please elaborate.

Reply

Student Three

Re: Re: Re: Discussion Week 2
Posted: Mon Feb 28 2011 04:31 PM

Ms. Ogletree,

Thank you for the distinction between the two, thinking maps and graphic organizers. I never thought about it like that before, but one other thing I realized, based on what you shared is that with the thinking map, the student is taking responsibility for THEIR thinking AND learning, whereas the graphic organizer has already been ORGANIZED FOR the student. I see the difference and will definitely plan to use it in my lessons next week. I will also share this with my team.

Reply

SECTION FIVE: INSTRUCTIONAL DESIGN METHODS USED WHEN TRANSITIONING TO A VIRTUAL LEARNING COMMUNITY

Presenting information involves the organization, formatting, and verbalization of knowledge delivered through technology tools. The tools should present the knowledge the teacher or user has co-constructed. The variability of Web 2.0 tools allows users to effectively present information that can be shared in the Learner–Learner model and keep the teachers fully engaged. As a district, we were in the process of being fully engaged in collaborative learning structures and building face-to-face professional learning communities. It was important that the instructional design support both collective and collaborative learning. Social networking tools embedded in the online learning platform provide excellent catalysts for this type of learning structure as well; the online platform must provide areas for discussion and feedback.

The users should demonstrate learning by analyzing their ideas, beliefs, and acquired information. Users should be guided to attempt to organize knowledge according to their unique experiences and interpretations. The structure of online professional development as well as the addition of Web 2.0 tools can benefit the learner in the organization and expression of knowledge developed, acquired, and shared in the virtual community using the Learner–Learner model.

Example: A participant (learner) logs in to the platform, selects a course to develop new skills and knowledge, learns new content in modules provided by the facilitator (learner), builds on this new knowledge with other participants and the facilitator with the same interests using engaging tools that allow them to collaborate and co-construct knowledge in a virtual community where they have access to each other and the content 24 hours a day! This process through the development of meaningful and relevant learning experiences supports higher-order thinking processes.

Concept development can be represented in a meaningful format through the interaction of information. Technology tools have allowed us open access to a wealth of information. Users must demonstrate effort and skill to acquire knowledge and began to construct new meanings and understanding from information. The creation of knowledge in a virtual learning community using the Learner–Learner model takes on a constructivist and social constructivist viewpoint.

We present information in modules. The number of modules depends on the content that is being taught, which guides the number of hours that will be reflected in the course. Some of the courses that have been offered are listed in the next section. In support of the Learner–Learner model, the courses flow as follows:

1. Content delivered in an engaging format using Web 2.0 tools that allow the teachers and the facilitator to share, build, and learn from each other

2. Activity/discussion related to content

3. Content delivered by facilitator and course participants in an engaging format and a process of collective collaboration

4. Activity/discussion related to content

5. Facilitator and participants follow up through sharing of strategies and lessons learned in reflection questions

Chunking the content is one best practice in online course design and development. Chunking the content is when the facilitator takes the big ideas of the skill being learned, synthesizes the information, and provides it in modules for the participants in the class. This allows the participants to access the content in sequence or out of sequence, depending upon their needs. The online environment gives them immediate access to the all the content at one time. Also, giving participants many opportunities to reflect on the material or complete a related task is a best practice that encourages internalizing of the concepts and keeping the learner engaged. Reflection gives the participants an opportunity to remain engaged in the learning process and have control over the path they take to differentiate and expand their learning based on personal goals. It also supports the collective process of learning for all the participants in the course, which creates the VLC environment.

As mentioned previously, our courses are designed to support teacher interests and district priorities. We use data to make these critical decisions. We also have a process of advertising the courses on our intranet system and through site-based communication. We are able to customize our courses where by developing content in the online platform, but we also use some of the tools and resources such as video links and discussion questions that are embedded in the platform and are designed by the vendor. The customization tools that are part of the online platform allow us to differentiate the courses to meet the needs of the all participants. As you will see from the listing of courses, we not only support and enhance learning for our teachers, but we have also designed courses to support administrators, bookkeepers, food-service employees, and substitutes. The beauty of the Web and our design provides for support of all the learners in our district. With the development of subject matter experts on the process of online pedagogy, we are able to diversify our course offerings with trained facilitators from all aspects of our organization. We currently have designed and offered more than 150 blended and online courses. The topics range from content development to personal development of teaching strategies and skills. Only 3 years ago, we started with 10. We have come a long way!

Twenty Courses From Several of Our Top Course Facilitators

1. Introduction to Interactive Notebooks

2. Engaging Activities to Promote Student Learning

3. Virtual Book Study: *The Fred Factor* and *Who Moved My Cheese?*

4. I Have Them in Groups; Now What?

5. What Effective Teachers Do Differently

6. The More Ways We Teach, the More Students We Reach

7. Integrating Technology Into Instruction: Virtual Classrooms

8. Technology Toolbox for Teachers

9. Elementary School Beginning of the Year Classroom Management

10. Foundations of Effective Math Teaching Strategies

11. Secondary Classroom Management: Understanding Student Needs

12. Differentiated Instruction

13. How to Communicate With Professionalism and Tact

14. Introduction to Teacher's Toolbox

SECTION SIX: THE ADVANTAGES OF A VIRTUAL LEARNING COMMUNITY

Online customized professional development opportunities have supported our ability to create and provide unique meaningful and engaging learning experiences for all district employees, with a specific emphasis on the teachers. The tools that support online professional development provide us the freedom to create differentiated learning experiences that are time sensitive and support the goals of the district.

The Advantages We Have Determined

Online Format. Unlike the purchase of materials, the online format allowed us to adjust our curriculum and target learning using current data and trends in education. We were able to integrate materials that were meaningful and demonstrated an impact on learning while developing additional tools to meet the gaps. Many of the courses are taught by teacher leaders. As they design their courses, they incorporate materials they have used n the classroom that have afforded them success with student performance. Books, instructional links, strategies, and ideas come directly from those who are in the field and can speak to the success of these resources that are highlighted and shared with the participants in the online course. In addition, participants who join the course also share their resources, strategies, and ideas through documents and videos that have proven to be successful in their classroom settings. The teaching profession often has teachers working in isolation. There are excellent examples of success, but we are not always able to benefit because of the time we spend in our classrooms. Online learning communities and tools provide participants with a time and place to collaborate and learn from each other.

Community of Learners. The tools also support collaboration among all the members of our district community of learners but allow them to adjust their time for learning according to their needs. We selected a platform that was easy to use, provided 24-hour access and system support, was easy to navigate for the end user, and allowed for customized creation of the content. Technology allows for synchronous and asynchronous learning environments, which allow for a variety of discussion and support from peers. The key is constant contact with the participants, which can take the form of responses to discussions, comments on work submitted, or even e-mails. Participants respond positively to colorful, positive e-mails with good graphics. We learn from the participants and they learn from us—collective learning. The discussions come to life through the Learner–Learner design. This learning environment supports our motto of "anytime, any place, at your own pace" learning.

Time. One of the most precious commodities in education is time. As expectations increase for students and for teachers, the days have not grown longer, but our list of to-dos has expanded. When is there time for adult learning? The use of online PD supported our ability to capture the time that was being lost and support job-embedded learning through school-based virtual learning communities. The participants also have the ability to access resources and tools long after they have completed this course, which saves them having to research these items when they need them in their classrooms.

Assessment. We are able to gain a general understanding of which courses are most requested through our ability to monitor use. Our collaborative discussion formats provide us monitored and recorded reflective feedback from participants, which supports our future decision making for classes to add, skills to develop, and overall general concerns about teaching and learning. The feedback allows us to take a close look at what does not work. We make ongoing improvements to our courses. The participants help us mold future courses.

Approval From Users. We have found that our users have reported high satisfaction with this format for professional learning. They particularly appreciate having access to their courses at any time that meets their scheduling preferences and needs. They like the collective thinking process they are engaged in with other members from the district. The course material is accessible to them to download, print, and save to their computers, unlike face-to-face sessions, at which they are given the handouts and often have to wait on professors to send the materials to them. This commitment to learning will empower the learning of district employees.

What Our Participants Say

The comments below demonstrate approval from end users. These are actual (unedited) comments collected at the end of courses. We maintain an archive of these comments, which we use to guide future classes and support continuation of funding. As you read through the comments, you can see that the structures that we carefully designed in support of our learners are exactly what they were looking for! They want a structure that supports their learning and collaboration in a community of learners. We also provide an online survey at the end of each course so that we can continue to evaluate the effectiveness of this structure of learning. Listed below are reflections from Mrs. Melissa Walker and Mrs. Natasha Rachell's courses. Mrs. Walker and Mrs. Rachell are online facilitators and have facilitated many of the courses for participants. They were coaches in the department and facilitated courses for teachers and other district participants. Their courses were always full and were frequently requested. They are integral contributors to our initial work and were trained in our facilitator's course. Prior to working in the department, they were high school math and science teachers. They currently work in another district and have been promoted to leadership positions in the field of instructional technology. The excerpts below are from an array of the courses they taught. Some of those courses are Introduction to Interactive Notebooks, Technology Tool Box for Teachers, Virtual Book Club: What Do Great Teacher Do Differently?, Differentiated Instruction, and How to Communicate With Professionalism and Tact.

> *"I really enjoyed the class and the freedom to do things from home helped tons. I will be using the information with my already kept visual journals when time allows it is hard with all the students from a school. I got plenty of information and look forward to sharing with others at my school."*

> *"A wealth of information was provided during the course so that I can begin to implement INs in my class."*

> *"I LOVED this class and have already begun to introduce the concept to my class!! I am so excited and so are my students. We will start November 1st. My instruction is interdisciplinary, so the notebook will be multi-subject and cover a variety of topics."*

> *"This course was extremely helpful. It opened my eyes to new strategies that can be implemented right away."*

> *"I plan to implement the different strategies weekly as I plan for instruction. My goal was to take away best practices for engaging students in today's classroom. It has been informative and a unique experience. I am leaving better equipped for the remainder of the year. I feel my toolbox has been added to and I am pleased with the use of my time during this class. Thank you for making it pertinent and useful. The course was indeed helpful."*

> *"I want to say thank you very much for the information that you presented in the course. It was excellent and I think I am very well prepared to challenge and engage the students this fall."*

> *"Thank you for an excellent course! The resources and materials provided were motivational, eye-catching, and extremely useful. Thank you for a well-planned and orchestrated course. Also, it was my first on-line course and I did enjoy it."*

"This has been a great course for me. I have learned a lot and have been able to aide my teachers with their lesson plans. I am able to give them ideas to keep the students motivated."

"Thank you for a challenging course. I felt I was in over my head at times, but it was a very positive experience. I can see how differentiation will make a big difference in the performance of my future students. Since we last met I received my GACE scores and passed the middle grades science exam. This class has helped to prepare me for my future classroom in ways I hadn't expected. There are so many options for differentiation that my mind was swimming at times, but you have provided resources we can use and practical exercises to familiarize us with them. I will use the tools gained from this course to reach as many of my students as possible."

"Great course. My first on line class, challenging, a bit intimidating, very informative and fun."

"The course was very useful. I think all employees should have an opportunity to learn these skills. I really enjoyed the accessibility of course. You have been very helpful to me. I've been able to update a few technical skills by taking this course. Thanks!"

"I thought this course was very useful. I enjoyed the ability to complete it at my own pace rather than a determined time. End-of-the-year activities are a little over whelming right now so being able to do the assignments on my own time frame was very beneficial. I liked the discussions. I would go back every few days and read what everyone was saying about the topic. A few times I gave feedback about what everyone was saying. Final thought, I think everyone would benefit from this course. I will be recommending it to all the teachers, etc. in my building. I already talked to my principal and AP about how good the course is in reference to our working environment."

5

Getting It Done

What Structures Support the Implementation of a Virtual Learning Community?

CORNERSTONE ONE: THE TECHNOLOGY-CENTRIC LEARNING ENVIRONMENT

The technology-centric learning environment supports the integration of technology for learning. A technology-centric environment successfully blends technology and learning strategies to advance user engagement and performance. The components of a technology-centric learning environment were supported by the structures below:

Online Curriculum/Course Designer. Added to the professional learning team was a professional teacher/administrator who had extensive knowledge in the area of instructional technology. It was important to have a designer who could blend both worlds (that of technology and that of instruction). Please see the work and technology leadership of Mrs. Henderson-Rosser infused throughout the structure of virtual professional learning communities.

Technology as a Tool for Learning. Instead of using the computers and other aspects of technology as pieces of hardware that house information or can be used to access information, we needed to shift the thinking about these tools as resources that would enhance learning and be the conduit to information acquisition. A technology-centric learning environment uses technology as a tool for learning. The participants have to understand access and use of electronic files and the power of the Internet to develop concepts. The computer without the use of constructs of social constructivist theory can be considered an electronic textbook, but the learning is dynamic and ever changing, and the technology-centric classroom uses the computer to access other resources and develop concepts as compared to using other teaching tools (textbooks, manipulatives, worksheets, etc.). Facilitation strategies are supported by the information that is accessed through the computer, including the structure of social networking tools to develop collaboration and a sense of community. We learn by doing and by being active participants! Just going through the process of taking online courses changes the adult learners' mind-set. We get to experience how to use videos to drive discussion, how to share our learning through Google documents, and how to model learning strategies through the use of videos and video journaling as well as how to reflect on our learning experiences through online discussions and participation in online professional networks. When teachers learn in a technology-centric environment, they can begin to visualize how to support learning through this format with their students.

The technology-centric environment allows for the learner to be independent and self-motivated while supporting a collaborative community. The online instructor in a technology-centric environment can become a guide on the side and is truly seen as a facilitator of learning. He or she should provide support so that learning will evolve through the participants. This aspect is very supportive of the Learner–Learner model of instructional design. The facilitator supports an environment in which the participants are engaged in developing an understanding of concepts independently and then co-construction of concepts with peers in the online community. This structure is designed to enhance their understanding and use of new skills using the computer or other mobile learning devices. Below is a list of examples of how technology supports learning cited by Robertson, Elliot, and Robinson (2007). Technology can motivate and engage learners through realistic contextual learning.

- Technology tools can help manage the work.
- Technology tools support diversified learners and various cognitive processes.
- Technology tools may support various functions simultaneously to support differentiation.
- Technology tools provide the ability to actively address meaningful questions and problem solving that are realistic and offer feedback.
- Technology tools allow users to focus on higher-order thinking and developing an array of knowledge through thinking and reflection.

In technology-centric learning environments for adult learners, technology tools are used to support the expression of knowledge. Professional learning that is structured to meet the needs of adult learners should consider two important aspects: self-directed learning and transformational learning experiences, discussed below.

Self-Directed Learning. The virtual learning community and the courses support self-directed learning. We were able to structure the selection of courses for differentiation, and with users being afforded the opportunity to complete coursework over a specified period in their own time, this is a clear benefit to the learning process that ultimately engages them in this type of learning. The participants manage their courses at their own pace, when it is convenient for them. Several courses have resources that allow teachers to dig deeper or engage in more research to add another level of enhancement to their learning and provide direction that meets their learning needs.

The course designer has created a full learning platform that is termed the PLeCampus. This has been done with the integration of all the courses that are offered in the virtual learning community. Now participants have many options to choose from while surfing in the PLeCampus.

Transformational Learning. The VLC provides participants with an opportunity to reflect on their learning and apply their skills in support of their learning needs. This process can be described as transformational. Transformative learning (TL) involves a profound shift in ways of being and knowing oneself and the world (Baumgartner, 2001). Different theorists look at TL through different lenses. Mezirow's (1991) most widely known theory emphasizes a cognitive process of *reflection on experiences,* assumptions, and beliefs leading to the adoption of a new perspective or changed view. The structure of your courses with an emphasis on collective collaboration and discussion fully supports the participants' reflection on their learning experiences as well as those of the other learners in the community.

CORNERSTONE TWO: ONLINE COURSE DESIGN—HOME GROWN

The use of technology as a tool for learning is a benefit to the success of online professional development. However, it should not overshadow the need for courses that are designed using national professional-development standards and support high-quality professional learning. One of the transitional points we found that provided a level of success is our transfer of well-designed, effective face-to-face courses to the online platform. We started this process through a blend so that we could communicate to our end users this shift of design and method of delivery. A blend is when we offer the initial class in a face-to-face model with the participants enrolled in the course. The remaining hours of facilitation are offered in the virtual learning community. This design was also reflective of the concern-based adoption model we had to take into consideration with this new way of offering courses.

Instructional design is one of the most critical aspects of your online professional development as well-designed content promotes successful learning. Most project managers will demand interactive and engaging online professional development, but they often confuse that with the technology "bells and whistles." Yes, online learning should be engaging to the senses, and there is media that can be very interactive and entertaining, but the biggest bang for your buck will result if your *content* is interactive and engaging. (Ross, 2011, p. 70)

It was important to determine if we would customize our content or use content from a variety of partner providers. Through careful review of many different online providers of content, we selected one that provided quality content but gave us the freedom to develop and customize courses and utilize courses that we had developed and implemented over the past several years. The design of our online community and courses was facilitated by our department's online course designer, Mrs. Henderson-Rosser. As the demand for classes grew, we developed a format for the development and training of additional facilitators and eventually designers of online courses. Again, Mrs. Henderson-Rosser was instrumental in this process.

Just like students, teachers need time to absorb new concepts, and they need access to ongoing support to implement the instructional strategies they gain from professional development. Led by this reality, our PD department began problem solving ways to increase our district's professional-learning capacity while maintaining or enhancing the quality of the training. We started off with a pilot process, and along the way, we requested feedback from teachers and facilitators. Teacher feedback along the way was crucial and provided true customization to the courses we develop. We continue to adjust the design to meet the needs of our users by offering courses in a format that was supported by them as well. We listened to our customers, and this process was a key to our success.

6

Building Capacity and Sustainability

School-Based Virtual Learning Cohorts

SECTION ONE: BUILDING CAPACITY

As the need and the interest for online courses grew, our online community was growing rapidly. However, we did not have the capacity to support the demand for this new way of learning. In support of building capacity, the online designer developed a course to train a cadre of facilitators. This online facilitator training course would allow master teachers, coaches, and administrators an opportunity to share strategies and content they had honed in their respective areas with our growing online community. (See Figure 6A for an outline of this course.) They would be taught how to become facilitators of online courses of their chosen subject matter. They learned how to create courses, infusing their unique skills into the courses and subject matter they teach.

We also developed virtual professional learning coaches. This structure of support was developed when we offered a blended model of Marzano's nine high-yield instructional strategies (Marzano, Pickering, & Pollock, 2001) training to every school system educator. We started with face-to-face training offered by a vendor (Teachscape), which provided an overview and training on Marzano's high-yield strategies to every principal and instructional coach in the district. We also purchased the book *Classroom Instruction That Works: Research-Based Strategies for Increasing Student Achievement* (Marzano, Pickering, & Pollock, 2001) for our district team members and virtual professional learning coaches in support of understanding and the development of Marzano's strategies. From this, our online course developer designed and customized virtual learning communities in our online platform for clusters of schools. The platform that we had chosen had preloaded content specific for Marzano's nine strategies. We used the material from the book and designed discussion groups and virtual learning communities around the content preloaded into the online platform.

During the training, a principal and instructional coach for each school were provided guidance on how to access the content in the platform and the process of being engaged in the virtual learning communities in clusters. In addition, we developed tools to guide them through this process that were loaded in a conference on our intranet system. With all of these tools and resources, we felt the need to have a virtual professional learning coach who was assigned approximately 25 to 30 schools and whose main role was to monitor the discussion that was developed from the reflective activities and provide ongoing support and feedback to each community of clusters. The identification and use of virtual professional learning coaches afforded a specific contact for each school when teachers and administrators responded to prompts and had questions regarding implementation of the new strategies they had learned from the Marzano's strategies training.

This structure allowed us to develop additional facilitators, and as a result, many courses were developed from this group of trained professionals. The virtual professional learning coaches were trained using the Online Facilitator course; see Figure

6A for the course outline. This course takes into consideration the standards of professional development that support high-quality professional-learning opportunities. It focuses on the principles embedded in adult learning theory and general online instructional design concepts as well as good basic teaching strategies that promote learning within a social and interactive context. Remember as you review, all of our online facilitators are teachers, instructional and academic coaches, administrators, bookkeepers, and dedicated, hard-working employees from the district. We know them to be subject matter experts and master educators. This course was designed to ensure that these skills could be developed by those who have the passion but did not necessarily have any history or background in online instruction. This model is great for schools and school systems that want to grow their own, which is the one of the most stable and viable examples of how to build capacity, sustainability, and scalability.

Section Two: School-Based Virtual Learning Cohorts

VLCs are very appropriate for district professional development; however, this model is also very suitable for schools. Schools are able to replicate this work through virtual learning cohorts. When teachers go to professional development courses as a single entity, they learn new skills, but unless they are expected to return and redeliver to the entire school, this new learning only impacts one classroom at the most. With the best intention, teachers return from conferences and are motivated to share their new learning with their colleagues, but there is no time for this to happen at the level and frequency that is required. A teacher learning in isolation does not support whole-school reform or a comprehensive plan for total school improvement.

During school-improvement planning, schools use data to determine schoolwide areas of focus for professional development. What happens when you are the principal and you don't have the budget to send all of your teachers to an individual conference or your district does not have the resources to provide the specific classes that your teachers need based upon your school data and the focal areas for your campus? Your budget does not support an expert coming to your school for one day at $3,500.00 a day. What happens? Generally, a well-developed plan is identified and turned in to the central office, and the principal shares with the staff that this needed skill development can be placed on next year's plan. Before you know it, you have a very disconnected process of developing your staff amid new mandates, changing standards, and processes that require you to develop effective teachers. It is not my intention to paint a bleak picture, but for many schools, this is the reality. When I was a principal, this was my reality. Even with the best intentions, the resources do not exist to support the professional-development goals that we determined based upon a good process of data analysis. Now what…so what?

One method of addressing this need is to implement school-based virtual learning cohorts. Most companies that sell online professional development platforms provide each site with a site license through which all staff at that site have access to all the tools and content in the platform. Most platforms come with a wealth of professional-development materials with embedded videos, journal articles, ebooks, and high-quality content on research-based areas of professional development, such as Marzano's nine high-yield strategies, classroom management, differentiated instruction, foundations of effective teaching in all the core content areas, and a host of essential teaching strategies. A school-based virtual learning cohort allows you to assign a specific topic for all of your teachers so they can engage in learning around the same topic. Your selected topics can all be aligned to your school-improvement goals. I have provided two examples of learning designs as examples that are shown in Figure 6B.

The school-based virtual learning cohort provides an opportunity for the teachers to come together around a variety of topics and co-construct new learning from sharing experiences and building upon new structures based upon new knowledge and new skills. Because there is 24-hour access, this learning can be scheduled over 3 to 4 months to allow for teachers to delve deeper into the content and integrate practice opportunities in between learning opportunities. It is also supportive of peer-to-peer observations and reflections. In order to support this structure, building leaders should determine teacher leaders who can serve in three primary roles: facilitator/learner, online course designer, and site-based professional learning leader.

This structure of learning in a VLC through school-based virtual cohorts is an excellent method of building capacity of knowledge and skills in your school, supporting and enhancing teacher effectiveness when teachers are provided continual improvement of instruction, and saving money and time, which are dwindling resources in our age of accountability and additional expectations. It will also move your teachers to 21st-century learning, in which the goal of having them learn in this format is to encourage them to use similar technology-centric tools when facilitating and teaching the students in their classrooms. This is a win-win for everyone!

Figure 6A

Topic of Learning	Design of Learning Virtual Learning Cohort
1. Classroom Management	1. Identify a facilitator. 2. Teachers meet in a blended model. 3. Teachers meet face-to-face to discuss the focus of the class and the topic. 4. Teachers meet in the online virtual learning cohort for the remainder of the time in their own place, space, and time! 5. Teachers engage in peer-to-peer observations.
2. Understanding Effective Math Questioning	1. Identify a facilitator. 2. Teachers participate in modules in online platform for effective math questioning. 3. Teachers participate in reflective practices around online content. 4. Teachers share, during a whole-group faculty meeting, suggestions for how they will integrate new learning into their classrooms. 5. Administrators conduct focused walk around math questioning techniques.

Figure 6B

Online Facilitator Course

Aleigha Henderson-Rosser

Module One: Online Orientation
Module Two: Welcome to the Professional Learning eCampus

a. Where Does eLearning Fit in Professional Learning?
b. Collaboration in eLearning
c. Learning Forward Standard of Professional Development

Module Three: Adult Learning Theory

a. Adults' Connection to the Learning
b. The Theory Behind Adult Learning
c. What Do You Know About Adult Learners?
d. More Theories to Consider for Adults

Module Four: Online Course Instructional Strategies

a. More Than Subject Matter Experts
b. Online Curriculum Interaction Model
c. Multiple Online Instructional Strategies—Choose Yours!
d. Conclusion—Online Instructional Strategies and Course Design

Module Five: Let's Get Started on Your Course

a. Professional Learning eCampus Employees—"Best Practices in Online Learning"
b. To Blend or Not to Blend—Blended Courses
c. Before You Begin Building Your Course
d. Library of Content
e. Instructional Matrices for Online Course Design
f. Best Practices in Online Instruction

Module Six: Tips and Tricks for the Online Instructor

a. Discussion Prompt Strategies
b. Blogs and Podcasts
c. Converting a Lecture Course to an Online Course

7

Pitfalls Don't Hold You Back

Over the past several years, we have had many celebrations due to the success of this design and structure. Our numbers of participants have increased dramatically. Our best marketing tool is word of mouth. Teachers are recommending the courses to their peers as well as venturing out and signing up for a variety of the courses. Until this current year, we had not had a concerted push to have participants learn using this design and format, and we continued to offer face-to-face courses that remained viable as a learning opportunity for our participants. However, for many who now prefer this format of learning, they see the value in the online courses, the virtual professional learning communities, and access to our full PLeCampus learning environment. We are excited because they continue to ask for more. Because there have been numerous requests for more, this year we have offered fewer face-to-face courses and have increased our effort to offer online courses in virtual learning communities. This was also a result of the continuation of budget and staffing cuts. We have fewer department members to offer face-to-face courses, and our teacher facilitators do not have the time to offer courses after school. Our current online platform provides an array of self-directed course opportunities that are engaging, relevant, and aligned to national, district, and school-based needs. In addition, the senior leadership view online professional development as a viable option to address the budget concerns. Therefore, we are all on the same page in planning to support our professional-development needs using the VLC format. It makes a difference when leaders plan together and consider the overall budget in this process.

We are also seeing benefits of the second-order change, in which our teachers who take these courses are starting to use technology and the Learner–Learner model with their students. We all know that it takes at least 5 years to see impact of a new structure. It is my belief that we are at the brink of a culture change and will see this option become the preferred option as 21st-century learning impacts the way our teachers learn as we are preparing for the impact it has on digital natives in our classrooms.

With our apparent success noted above, there remain cultural changes we must overcome. As we know, the adult learners during this period of the 21st century are mostly digital immigrants, so the world of online learning is something new for most of us. Overcoming the fear of the unknown, especially if one has little technical skill, has some participants apprehensive about taking online courses. Word of mouth has been the best method to help colleagues overcome this fear. However, on our end, making sure to provide extreme patience and treat "newbies" with kid gloves has helped give the online courses a good reputation. Teachers are extremely busy after school, and it is difficult for them to attend a meeting at a remote location after school ends. One of the values observed in the online process is the management of time. However, for our newbies, the one face-to-face meeting calms the fear of this being a new way of doing things and the belief that they are not prepared to take on this new type of learning. We have seen a better response with these participants from having the initial face-to-face meeting online. Overall, most participants appreciate being able to take their course 100% online. Needless to say, I am excited to see us transition to offering additional online opportunities for learning.

WHAT WERE THE PITFALLS? HOW DID WE OVERCOME THEM?

The process of developing the Learner–Learner model of online professional development afforded us many successes, but we experienced some clear challenges.

The Vision. Communicating the vision to all stakeholders requires cross-collaboration of departments, roles, and responsibilities. This is a collaborative process that will require the support of your senior leadership staff, professional-development designers, subject matter experts, and teachers.

Hiring or Collaborating With a Person Skilled in Instructional Technology. It is imperative to have someone who understands instructional technology or has an inherent love for using technology as a tool for learning on board in this process. We secured a dedicated person to support the development of this process. However, if you have a technology support specialist, instructor, or passionate teacher who has received the training or has the skill to design this structure to support the adult learning model presented above, you have all you need. The basic premise is transference of 21st-century learning for your adult learners and making this effort a collaborative effort. It is the same process we are now using for students.

Shift of Roles and Responsibilities. Until we realized the need to train facilitators and create virtual professional-learning coaches, I depended solely on the curriculum/online course designer. Once online professional learning becomes a priority, you will need to take a close look at your current structure of roles and responsibilities for the members of your organization. It will be imperative to adjust the roles and responsibilities of current members in your organization so that you have dedicated time to developing the new initiative of online professional learning. As well, you will need to have staff that is able to serve in a capacity to fulfill your goal of creating a virtual professional learning community. The online course designer was promoted to a new position and district last year. However, this did not compromise our use of online professional development. We have continued to use this professional-learning design and increased the number of participants. Because this was a collaborative effort of district leaders and department members, it did not depend on one team or one person. However, the vision could not have been fulfilled without the passion and dedication of the original builders and designers of this process.

Using What We Had Available to Us. Initially, we were seeking videos that supported our courses. As we journeyed through this search, I realized that we would incur a financial commitment that we could not afford. Part of this process is doing an assessment of what you have. As stated previously, this process is not designed to add an increase to your budget. Most districts and organizations have the resources they need to design a platform that supports this structure. It remains critical for us to customize our courses from the resources we have instead of looking outside the organization. As well, we trained and developed our human resources so that they could be a viable part of transforming our learning environments and saving money. We trained our district and school staff (coaches, teachers, administrators) on how to become online facilitators and subject matter experts. We did not hire new people or bring in consultants to do this work for us. We also took materials that we had used in our face-to-face courses and transferred them to an online environment. There was no need to buy new materials. We used Web 2.0 tools that are free and available on the Internet. We did not have to buy software packages to support the learning structure in our VLCs. Because the courses are online, we saved money on physical resources such as facility use and payment of plant managers to lock up the building and provide custodial services. The benefits of bringing teachers together from all schools through technology in the virtual learning community saved them gas money and valuable time.

Selecting a Platform. There were and still remain many available online platforms or course management systems, also known as learning management systems, that support virtual learning communities. Some of the platforms available are School Improvement Network's PD 360, Teachscape, Association for Supervision and Curriculum Development (ASCD) PD

Online, and True North Logic, to name a few. These platforms come loaded with research-based content in core subjects and instructional strategies that provide a good foundation for your courses. There are also free online platforms such as Moodle and Edmodo, which educators use to create effective online and social networking sites for students and teachers and build their own content and learning communities. These are great alternatives that provide a great start, but they will require that you develop your own courses. We spent a great deal of time searching for the option that worked best for our district. However, some of the other departments were using other platforms. There was a period of time during which we were not on the same page and had to collaborate on our efforts and use of financial resources in support of district priorities. In the end, we all agreed that we needed to secure a online learning platform that we could afford, and equally important was the ability to customize our current work instead of replacing it with canned online courses that the vendor offered with the platform. Since we started this process, technology has continued to advance, and there are now numerous options. Take the time to go through this step and choose the option that works best for your district and supports your budget.

Negotiating With Online Partner Providers. Many of the online platform providers or partners have great products to offer. Some platforms are full of resources that you may not need for the price, and some do not have enough and their product will not meet your needs. In most instances, they are willing to provide some level of product customization in support of your school's or district's needs. Instead of purchasing all that they have to offer, select those tools that will benefit your learning environment the most and will support the resources that you have (financial and human) to dedicate to this learning structure. Taking the time to meet the vendors and view the options is a critical part of the selection process. This is by far one of the greatest successes we experienced in this entire journey; however, it is a step that must not be compromised in order to gain the benefits you are seeking in support of your priorities. I do not use the word *partner* lightly. The vendor should seek to support your needs and provide modifications in the design if doing so will support your goal of providing online professional development to your participants.

Securing Funding for a Platform. Many of the other departments in our district were using other online platforms that were meeting their immediate needs. In order to implement this process districtwide, it was necessary for us to merge funding for professional learning so that we could obtain a full suite of what was needed to develop and implement the online virtual learning community. Initially, there was little to no collaboration with other departments; however, once the connections were made and the collaboration was supported, we were able to save money and meet the needs of more personnel.

Growing Your Own Online Courses. As the interest for online learning grew among our users, the need increased for us to have additional persons to support this mode of learning. Our demand was presented before our supply. The development of an online facilitator's course was born out of the need to increase our offerings and support the needs and interests of users. It would be beneficial to provide this resource when starting this initiative.

Increase in Funding. As demand increased, the need for funding increased. We made budget adjustments during the year to accommodate the demand. If funding is available, plan in advance and provide funding for all the resources that will be required. The adjustment was made by moving money from other categories in which it was no longer needed, such as books, supplies, instructors, and consultants. Materials are embedded in the online structure and need not be supplied separately. However, it would be beneficial to make the necessary shifts to the budget in the initial stages of implementation. It is always best to start small so that you can monitor the need for additional funding and collect data on usage to support the funding request.

How Do We Keep the Momentum Going? As the demand grew for additional courses and district initiatives in support of this structure, we needed to ensure that our online facilitators were developed and the users were provided with the support required in a reflective online community. The development of the virtual professional-learning coaches was a powerful enhancement to this process. Our virtual professional-learning coaches were pulled from our current staff of instructional coaches. In addition, we provided an open call to master teachers who were providing levels of guidance to their peers in areas of instructional strategies and content development through school-based professional learning as well as serving on district-based cadres in specific subjects. They became a pool of subject matter experts. Because we have an online facilitator training module and class, we have been able to develop virtual professional-learning coaches from this pool of dedicated educators. Besides this being a demonstration of how we keep the momentum going, it also provides a level of differentiated professional development for our master teachers and continues to increase our pool of teacher leaders. We also use our district content coordinators in curriculum and instruction as facilitators.

How Do We Assess the Impact on Student Learning? This is still by far our biggest challenge. We have a good handle on assessment of teacher learning and practices. However, we have yet to venture into having a clear plan for consistently assessing the impact on student learning. We have some facilitators who start action research projects with some of the users of their courses, and the participants in those courses are asked to share feedback and data on student performance. The majority of this reporting is based upon observation and reflection of what the teacher observes in his or her classroom after implementing the strategies. Our next focus of work is how we can determine the impact that participant learning in the virtual learning communities has on student learning through the review of documented student performance and achievement results. The questions we are yet to fully answer with a direct correlation to our virtual communities are as follows: Are the participants learning new skills that will improve their teaching effectiveness? Are students improving academically because of the teacher's learning in courses that are offered in these virtual learning communities? We are in the process of designing a full management system to capture through video the delivery of instructional strategies embedded in our teacher-evaluation system. Along with this work comes the ability for the teacher to upload artifacts and data in support of his or her recorded classroom session with the students. It is our hope that this will lead to targeted professional development as well as support for student performance based upon teacher delivery of specific strategies learned in the online or face-to-face professional-learning course. Each teacher will be provided with a growth plan with identified goals and objectives that are tied to teacher evaluation and student standards of learning. This work will require a great deal of teacher management and administrator review. With the onset of many other required mandates for school-based and district staff, this will initially feel like an added requirement to already busy schedules. Part of this work is demonstrating how it replaces what is currently being done instead of being an addition and how this process can and will streamline the work through a system of electronic and online management. We will keep you posted on this work, but we feel certain that it can be done.

8

Summary

My Reflections

This work is really about providing the education community of adult learners with a techno-centric 21st-century learning process as they engage in professional development throughout their careers. The Learner–Learner model supports this type of learning because it proposes that the facilitator of learning is in symbiotic learning relationship with the receiver of learning. This is can be easily accomplished through technology. The format of a virtual professional learning community provides a structure through which the learner is in control of his or her learning. The facilitator sets the stage, but the learner can become engaged in activities that guide and develop his or her performance. In addition, the learners engage with others who have the same or similar interests and can capitalize on this relationship any time of the day, no matter where they are geographically. As educators, we are making great strides when it comes to offering this type of learning for our students. However, we have forgotten about the key players who make it happen for the students.

It is my belief that this type of learning for teachers will transfer to the classrooms at a level we have never experienced before. A great deal of research has been done on the fact that teachers teach the way they learn. If we don't offer opportunities for them to learn in this format, our desire to see them teach students in a techno-centric learning environment will be challenging to fulfill. Let's face it, the majority of us digital immigrants have been working in isolation and in silos. Outside of traditional meetings that bring us together for one-shot opportunities, we rarely communicate to each other on the magical opportunities that are exhibited in our students in our schools, classrooms, and districts every day. Online virtual learning communities will pull us out of that structure and offer a professional network that erases the barriers that we have lived with and worked within for years.

In my world, we are not yet where I know we can be. However, online virtual learning communities have been the best answer for pulling our educators—who, by the nature of our district's size, can go an entire career and never have the opportunity to speak with or meet a peer who bears the same responsibility, the same passion, but is on the other side of town. However, this process of isolation can and does happen with teachers who are across the hall from each other! It excites me when I can go into one of the virtual learning communities we have built and, in an instant, feel the pulse of the great teaching that is happening across the district but at the same time have a clear picture of what we continue to struggle as I read the reflections that are shared in support of development, improvement, and engagement.

My hope is that virtual learning communities can be facilitated all over the world and that schools, districts, and learning organizations continue to connect in this structure. The Learner–Learner model fully supports the fact that we really are socially connected through learning and can benefit from each other. My journey was born out of need to make sure that the human element of learning is not taken away by the use of technology. In our current world, in which time is as important a resource as money, we could find an engaging way to give that gift back to each other through the advances that technology brings us.

Finally, if we can do this, I know that you can, too. I hope this guide will be the catalyst that will jump-start your journey of transforming your face-to-face professional learning communities into virtual learning communities. In addition, we have designed a platform in which the Learner–Learner model is actualized in all learning environments.

If you are interested in starting a plan and taking that journey to the next step, please do not hesitate to contact us. We are here to partner with you.

Virtually yours,
Dr. Sonja Hollins-Alexander
Mrs. Aleigha Henderson-Rosser

References

Barth, R. (2006). Improving relationships within the school house. *Educational Leadership, 63*(6), 8–13.

Baumgartner, L. M. (2001). An update on transformational learning. In S. B. Merriam (Ed.), *New directions for adult and continuing education: No. 89. The new update on adult learning theory* (pp. 15–24). San Francisco: Jossey-Bass.

Bolden, L. (2008, June 22). *Adult learning paper receives TNF Scholarly Writing Award: making a case for andragogical approaches to teaching and mentoring Students The Free Library.* Retrieved February 27, 2011, from http://www.thefreelibrary.com/Adult learning paper receives TNF Scholarly Writing Award: making a...-a0185655403

Boyd, V. (1992). *School context. Bridge or barrier to change?* Austin, TX: Southwest Educational Development Laboratory.

Chickering, A. W., & Gamson, Z. F. (1987). Seven principles for good practice in undergraduate education. *Wingspread Journal, 9*(2), 1. [See also AAHE Bulletin, March 1987.]

Danielson, C. (2009). *Talk about teaching!: Leading professional conversations.* Thousand Oaks, CA: Corwin.

Derry, S. J. (1999). A fish called peer learning: Searching for common themes. In A. M. O'Donnell & A. King (Eds.), *Cognitive perspectives on peer learning* (pp. 197–211). Mahwah, NJ: Lawrence Erlbaum.

Ernest, P. (1991). *Social constructivism as a philosophy of mathematics: Radical constructivism rehabilitated? Psychology of mathematics education* (Vol. 1). New York: Department of Science Teaching, Weizmann Institute of Science.

Gredler, M. E. (1997). *Learning and instruction: Theory Into practice* (3rd ed.). Upper Saddle River, NJ: Merrill.

Hall, G. E., & Hord, S. M. (1987). *Change in schools: Facilitating the process.* New York: State University of New York Press.

Hord, S., & Sommers, W. (2009). *Leading professional learning communities.* Thousand Oaks, CA: Corwin.

Hord, S. M., Rutherford, W. L., Huling-Austin, L., & Hall, G. E. (1987). *Taking charge of change.* Alexandria, VA: ASCD.

Joyce, B., & Showers, B. (1980). Improving inservice training: The messages of research. *Educational Leadership, 37*(5), 379–385.

Kapp, A. (1833). Die Andragogik ober Bildung im mannlichen Alter. *Platons Erziehungslehre, als Pädagogik für die Einzelnen und als Staatspadagogik.* Germany: Minden und Leipzig.

Knowles, M. S. (1973). *The adult learner: A neglected species.* Houston, TX: Gulf Publishing Company. Revised edition 1990.

Knowles, M. S. (1980). *The modern practice of adult education; from andragogy to pedagogy* (Rev. ed.). Chicago: Follett.

Kukla, A. (2000). *Social constructivism and the philosophy of science.* New York: Routledge.

Lave, J., & Wenger, E. (1991). *Situated learning. Legitimate peripheral participation.* Cambridge, UK: University of Cambridge Press.

Learning Forward. (2011). *Standards for professional learning.* Oxford, OH: Author.

Louis, K. S., & Kruse, S. D. (1995). *Professionalism and community: Perspectives on reforming urban schools.* Thousand Oaks, CA: Corwin.

Marzano, J. M., Pickering, D. J., & Pollock, J. E. (2001). *Classroom instruction that works: Research-based strategies for increasing student achievement.* Alexandria, VA: Association for Supervision and Curriculum Development.

McMahon, M. (1997, December). *Social constructivism and the World Wide Web—a paradigm shift for learning.* Paper presented at the ASCILITE conference, Perth, Australia.

Mezirow, J. (1991). *Transformative dimensions in adult learning.* San Francisco: Jossey-Bass.

National Staff Development Council. (2001). *Standards for staff development.* Retrieved December 3, 2011, from http://www.nsde.org/standards/index.cfm

Prawat, R. S., & Floden, R. E. (1994). Philosophical perspectives on constructivist views of learning. *Educational Psychologist, 29*(1), 37–48.

Robertson, B., Elliot, L., & Robinson, D. (2007). Cognitive tools. In M. Orey (Ed.), *Emerging perspectives on learning, teaching, and technology.* Retrieved January 27, 2013, from http://projects.coe.uga.edu/epltt/

Ross, J. D. (2011). *Online professional development: Design, deliver, succeed.* Thousand Oaks, CA: Corwin.

Schunk, D. H. (2000). Social cognitive theory. In K. M. Davis (Ed.), *Learning theories: An educational perspective* (3rd ed., p. 118). Upper Saddle River, NJ: Merrill.

Tate, M. (2004). *Sit & get won't grow dendrites: 20 instructional strategies that engage the adult brain.* Thousand Oaks, CA: Corwin.

Vygotsky, L. S. (1978). *Mind in society: The development of higher psychological process.* Cambridge, MA: Harvard University Press.

Index

CORWIN

A SAGE Company

The Corwin logo—a raven striding across an open book—represents the union of courage and learning. Corwin is committed to improving education for all learners by publishing books and other professional development resources for those serving the field of PreK–12 education. By providing practical, hands-on materials, Corwin continues to carry out the promise of its motto: **"Helping Educators Do Their Work Better."**